Praise for Dino Watt

"Dino is a master communicator AND teacher! He understands the steps to build trust, confidently present, overcome obstacles and achieve desired results and he brilliantly implements these steps enrolling others to learn his process. Whether you're selling on-screen or in-person you will love what you learn and how much better your consults become because of your improved connections and communication." - **Dr. Scott Law- Orthodontist, Smile Doctors CCO**

"Dino Watt is a giant in our industry.

Not only do I highly recommend the importance of this work from cover to cover but to follow him to absorb the many gifts and skills he provides us.

He is personally passionate and committed to make a difference and we are fortunate that he chose dentistry and are the better for it." - **Dr. Lou Shuman DMD CAGS, Cellerant Consulting Group**

"This book is awesome. Whether you are a "virtual veteran" or just dipping your toes in the teledentistry pool, this book is a must read. Dino not only presents the concepts of virtual exams and practical reasons why we should be doing so very clearly, he takes it a step further and provides the reader with some concrete tips on getting these systems in place right away. Share it with your treatment coordinator or sales representative to get them on board, too!" - **Dr. Tom Marcel, Marcel Orthodontics**

"Modern patients and parents are continually adopting technologies that optimize for their time. Virtual consults are a great way to meet the patients where they are today. Dino has a clear passion for translating the patient's mindset into a clinical workflow that is both practical and efficient. He has masterfully done it again here for virtual consult integration, and this is a must read for those practices who want to keep moving forward." - **Dr. Alfred Griffin, Orthodontists, Lightforce Founder and CEO**

"Dino Watt is a pioneer! His vision and unrelenting quest to help practitioners grow their practice and help them work less and enjoy life more is his passion. He is at the forefront of new technology and leading the charge of change within the dental industry. His new book Mastering Virtual Exams is a game changer! When most practices were struggling with the shutdown during the Covid Pandemic, Dino doubled down on virtual exams and helped his clients thrive during this unprecedented time. He is the real deal and his new book will change your career and practice life forever." - **Dr. Stuart Frost, Frost Orthodontics**

"Dino Watt has the uncanny ability to connect to his audience, at large in person conferences, live one on one coaching, or through the computer. He has distilled these unique skills into a powerful and effective masterpiece which will undoubtedly give you the tools to connect to your patients through the computer and start more patients without them even entering your office. Turning one of the most challenging hurdles in sales, to the biggest boom in your practice. We have implemented Dino's techniques at Prero Orthodontics and have seen a remarkable return on investment. I highly recommend this book to give you tools to connect with your virtual and in person consultations. A must read for everyone in the office to increase your ability to connect with others and create more smiles. Dino Watt shines bright like lightning." - **Dr. Dovi Prero, Prero Orthodontics**

"No matter how long you've been practicing or how many years your treatment coordinator has been working, this is a must-read book for both of you. The tips and concepts Dino shares can help anyone get better engagement with patients for higher case acceptance and lower stress throughout the new patient process." - **Dr. Glenn Krieger, Krieger Orthodontics, Orthopreneurs**

"Dino has led the charge for virtual selling and this book should become required reading for anyone in orthodontic practice." - **Dr. James Reynolds, Spillane & Reynolds Orthodontics**

"We live in a world where everything is "On Demand." The shows we watch, the food we eat for dinner, the groceries we buy from the store and the clothes we wear can all be purchased with the click of a few buttons. We also live during a time of education overload on social media when it comes to different procedures and outcomes. People want full transparency of your process and pricing without having to get a babysitter, take time off work and drive across town to spend an hour in your chair to get their questions answered and the technology is available today to give people exactly what they want. If you are not doing virtual appointments already, start doing it NOW! It is the single best thing I have ever done for my practice and has allowed me to do more of the dentistry I love to do. As Mark Cuban says, "Make your product easier to buy than your competition or you will find your customers buying from them and not you." - **Dr. Brain Harris, Virtual Smile**

"I have been in the orthodontic world for over 30 years. I can honestly tell you I have gotten more out of the information in this book than any other. It's not just about virtual appointments. It's about how to communicate better as a TC, as a business owner, heck, as a person. Do yourself a favor and read it, then, have your whole team read it. You will be grateful you did." - **Nic Bradfield, Owner OTG Consulting**

"I just love Dino Watt. We first crossed paths at a conference a few years ago, and I was immediately struck by his authenticity and his generosity. He's one of those people that just wants to help you, help your business, and help the world become a better place. And when it comes to understanding how people interact, both personally and professionally, he's one of the best in the game. At Straight Consulting, we've been beating the drum the last few years about the generational impact that Millennials will have on the industries they touch, much as their Baby Boomer predecessors had before them. If businesses, ortho or otherwise, are going to effectively serve these Millennials, they HAVE to be willing to adapt and meet these consumers where they are. And for Generation Y, that means on the go, mobile, and

virtually. Dino's call to master virtual consults isn't just a "nice to have" for the next decade plus of consumers, it's critical. It's time to evolve, or face extinction, and this book is a perfect way to help you do it!" - **Tracy Martin, Straight Consulting, Ortho Evolution**

"Dino is the truest, most authentic and passionate trainer I've ever met! He wants YOU to live your best life, both personally and professionally. He's got the tools for you to do just that and in his humorous and genuine way, he demonstrates how to make the changes to grow and improve! During a time when our world gave us no option but to adjust our processes to serve our patients, Dino was ahead of the wave in how to do it and has provided you with the information needed to be as successful as possible in this journey. In his book, "Master Virtual Exams", Dino helps you to see your process from an updated and progressive viewpoint that will truly set you and your practice apart!" - **Michelle Shimmin, International lecturer, training and consultant Owner Shimmin Consulting**

MASTERING
VIRTUAL CONSULTS

CONNECT, COMMUNICATE AND CLOSE
NEW PATIENTS THROUGH THE SCREEN.

DINO WATT

ISBN: 978-1-64184-668-4 (Paperback)
ISBN: 978-1-64184-669-1 (Ebook)

Contents

Foreword ix

Introduction xiii

Chapter 1: A new opportunity reveals itself. 1

Chapter 2: Beginning with the end in mind 17

Chapter 3: Your sales personality and selling to theirs. 44

Chapter 4: What every body is saying 73

Chapter 5: Words that tell and words that sell 114

Chapter 6: Building the Case 140

Chapter 7: Closing the Deal 164

Chapter 8: Advanced Sales Skills 192

Afterword. 217

My Virtual Start. 221

Dino's Best Reads. 223

Foreword

Before I reached out to Dino Watt, my back was up against the wall.

I am a master of sales, earning multiple 7-figures onstage myself and having researched and taught sales for decades. I had just launched a new book, *D.R.I.V.E. Sales: The 5 Secrets to Increase Sales by 400%*, which organically hit #1 on Amazon during its first week. I had been asked to present my methods to a worldwide audience and was flying out to meet the film crew. There was only one problem: a small concern from a continent away which had grown into a monster, threatening to swallow the sales industry whole.

Covid had hit. For my audience of commissions-based sales professionals, the pandemic was like a gut punch. In a matter of days, their offices were shuttered, their calendars wiped clean and their potential clients had hidden themselves at home. Massive sales events, the bread-and-butter of the industry, were cancelled and the stages used to promote their businesses lay in darkness before empty auditoriums. With no way to get in front of potential clients, many people in sales watched helplessly as their bank accounts ran dry and the quarantine kept extending from days to weeks to months.

How was I going to present in front of this demoralized sales audience? I had full confidence in my methods, having built five separate million-dollar companies, but had no idea how to help people connect with their clientele during a pandemic. That's when I thought of Dino Watt.

Nine years ago I met Dino Watt and we made a lasting connection. When Covid first hit, I had seen him on social media, actively reaching out with his clients and offering solutions for selling on-screen. I knew I needed what he had, so in those few days before my global presentation, I sent him a message. He gave me full access to his Selling Through the Screen course with content geared towards on-screen presentation, body language, connecting with powerful words, and a simple guide for creating a quality at-home virtual studio. I binge-watched every single video in his modules and was able to use his virtual sales expertise to give both actionable tools and some solid hope to my sales audience during the presentation.

His training is hands-down the best I have seen for connecting through the screen. I had found my mentor, and the wisdom he imparted has been a lifeline for me.

A few weeks later, Dino reached out to let me know that he had just devoured my book cover-to-cover during a business conference. We talked about his upcoming projects and realized how well our content dovetailed together, complementing without competing. The D.R.I.V.E. Sales System offers you an understanding of your own sales drive, validating who you are internally while also allowing you to be more authentic in the external world. It pairs beautifully with Dino's wisdom on virtual sales. I offered him the rights to publish my sales system as a chapter in this book and sent him the full manuscript of D.R.I.V.E. on the spot (you'll read more about the D.R.I.V.E. Sales System in chapter 3).

If you are a veteran of the sales coaching industry, you know that this type of collaboration never happens. We've been able to create this relationship of trust because Dino Watt is the real deal. So many personalities have an onstage persona and then they become someone else when the spotlight turns off, but Dino is the same guy on and off the stage. He's one of the most authentic people I have ever met.

Recently I hosted a three-day Mega Mansion Mastermind sales retreat at a 25,000-square-foot estate. Using Dino's virtual sales techniques, I was able to sell out my high-ticket-price event within 24 hours and increase my sales by 327%. I invited Dino to fly out and teach at the event, and then something happened that has never been a problem in all of my decades of speaking experience: I lost my voice. There I was, hosting all of these people who had paid multiple thousands of dollars to spend a few days with me, and I was losing my ability to speak. Right away, I texted Dino and asked him to step up. I tried bumping his presentation up to allow my voice to recover, but my ability to speak got progressively worse. By the end of breakfast on that first day I knew I was in trouble. I asked him to pinch-hit the event for me, and the master once again stepped up in a big way. He hosted that entire retreat. I would pull up my visuals on the screen and whisper to him what content I wanted him to focus on, and he took my information and ran with it. Disaster was averted and the retreat was a massive success, sealing the deal for me as a raving fan of Dino Watt. I love this man. I would do anything for him.

Dino Watt is a visionary and a key player in the resurrection of the entire sales industry. His ability to consume complex information and simplify it for the masses is a sign of true genius. As Einstein put it, "Genius is making complex ideas simple, not making simple ideas complex." Dino Watt's simple, relevant tools and insights will revolutionize your business, and now is the time to do it.

I believe 100% that the principles taught in *Mastering Virtual Exams* will be the most important insights this decade because consumers everywhere now demand on-screen sales options. Communication in business will never retrogress back to where it was before. Virtual sales can be used not just to survive, but to scale your business in the #1 most effective way. While every principle in this book also applies to face-to-face sales, Dino Watt will teach you the keys of selling virtually, a technique that nobody else is teaching. As we come full circle from the chaos of the pandemic, his work will be instrumental in the reemergence of the industry.

You have found your virtual sales mentor! Allow Dino Watt to enable you to bring what you do best to an ever-expanding audience, selling through the screen at a higher level. His work will help you reconnect to more people while simultaneously deepening your connection to yourself.

-Woody Woodward, CEO, D.R.I.V.E. Sales System

Introduction

"The Chinese use two brush strokes to write the word 'crisis.' One brush stroke stands for danger; the other for opportunity. In a crisis, be aware of the danger — but recognize the opportunity."

-John F. Kennedy

It happened without warning. Remember when the world stopped? One morning you woke up and went about your day as usual with work, school and commitments, and the very next day all of that had ceased. March of 2020. Suddenly, everything was cancelled, and the weeks turned into months. There were times of fear, anxiety about the future, loss. But there were also unexpected moments of clarity in the stillness. There was an increased focus on what was truly working in our lives, and there were other things we found we weren't missing out on at all. It was a powerful time. It was out of this moment when the world stopped that this work was born.

The world has stopped before. When the Great Plague threatened London in 1665, Cambridge University closed its doors and Isaac Newton was forced to stay home. It was during this time that he invented calculus and imagined optic theory. Allegedly, while sitting in his garden, he watched an apple fall from a tree. This image inspired his understanding of gravity and the laws of motion. When the world slowed down, Newton thrived. The year he spent in quarantine was later referred to as the "year of wonders."

Newton didn't stop thinking when the world stopped. He continued to imagine, observe and invent. He stayed the course, continuing his education, but changed his plans to learning outside of the university environment. We likewise can retain our vision. We simply have to change our strategies to adapt to what is. There is opportunity in the midst of uncertainty.

World-changing businesses start during recessions. Layoffs lead to new careers, sometimes careers that people never before considered but that end up becoming far more fulfilling than what they were doing before. If you've always wanted to work remotely, now you have the chance. If you're self-quarantining somewhere, how can you emerge with a new book, podcast, album, work of art, or just a big idea? It's time to get comfortable with being uncomfortable. Good things will happen in the midst of the chaos.

Many industries have been on the edge of a shift toward virtual interaction for so long, and this pandemic has been a massive catalyst for that movement. Learning to sell in a virtual environment is essential right now.

Consider the story of the owners of Netflix meeting with executives at Blockbuster. Netflix was experiencing growing pains and offered to sell to Blockbuster for $50 million. The Blockbuster leadership laughed them out of the room, reasoning that their clientele liked the in-store model and wouldn't want to go online. They thought people valued going to the store to socialize. But it turns out that socializing is not what people want when it comes to entertainment. Turns out that people just want to sit in their underwear, eat ice cream, and watch exactly what they want to watch.

Going to the mall makes no sense when you can shop for anything you could possibly need, and a bunch of things that you don't really need, on Amazon. The reason Uber is dominating the taxi market isn't because it's a novel way to hire a taxi. Uber dominates because they are giving people their time back. Right now, the strongest businesses all interact with their clients virtually. What if this pandemic is not the force that stunted your industry, but the catalyst for doing even better business that clients will love even more? Selling through the screen is the future, and the future is here.

I've been selling online since 2010. I was in the training and coaching industry and spent a lot of time in airplanes and on the road. I loved the work but had small kids at home and often felt torn between work and family. I decided to make some changes to my model so I could be with my family more. For many years now, other than speaking engagements and the occasional in-person office visit, my business has been operating fully online. Over that decade, I've been able to master the art of selling through the screen. I've sold hundreds of courses and packages, from a couple thousand dollars all the way up to six figures, to clients I have never been in the same room with.

I know what I'm doing. I'm sharing this part of my story with you because I want you to feel confident in my expertise. This book includes challenges for you to implement at the end of each section. I'm going to ask you to do business differently than you have ever done it before. As a coach, my job is to push you, so you are going to have to push yourself.

Each of you are at a different level when it comes to your presence online. I know many of you work in dentistry and orthodontics because I train in that space a lot, but these tools will work across many industries. You may have been conducting business virtually for a while and feel pretty seasoned, and I know there are others who are afraid to make a video. Most of you will fall somewhere in between. Wherever you are, you're holding the right book. You'll learn techniques that can help you get started or help you finesse and master virtual exams.

I do have one caution for you involving mindset. I've learned that in any educational setting, the most dangerous thing a student can be thinking is, "I know that!" Holding this phrase in your mind will shift your focus and stop your growth. As you read these selling techniques, I want you to be aware of your thoughts. Hear yourself!

You are a top performer and you care about growth or you wouldn't be reading this. There might be some things presented that you have heard before. So when you find yourself thinking, "I already know that one," think instead, "How can I learn more about this? How can I re-position this? How can I bring this idea more fully into my business?"

There is a huge difference between common understanding and common practice. These are two drastically different things, but human beings often mistake one for the other. For example, to lose weight it is common knowledge that you need to eat less and move more. Simple: eat less and move more. Everybody knows this — I know I'm not dropping a truth bomb on you right now. We all know it. It's the practicing that trips us up. So keep an open mind as you are reading. Don't let what you have heard before get in the way. Sometimes it is the simple truths, re-imagined, that are the most powerful.

1

A new opportunity reveals itself

D r. Jim Lupi opened Lupi Orthodontics in the greens of Virginia over two decades ago. His business is successful not only because of the great work and quality care he gives his patients, but also because he has built a team of dedicated and passionate professionals who are the backbone of the business.

When Covid-19 hit, Jim knew he needed to adapt. Although we had previously discussed how he could use virtual technology to manage his schedule better for non-essential in-office appointments like retainer checks or growth guidance appointments, it was not something he was focused on before the shutdown. Like most of his colleagues, worry and concern over the future of his business was high. Legally, he could no longer see patients in the office, so he knew he needed to set up a system so his team could connect with patients virtually. He knew if he could get even a few people to hold virtual appointments and if he could close a small percentage of them, it was better than doing nothing at all.

His treatment coordinator, Kim, quickly dove into learning all she could about how to connect, communicate and close new patients via a virtual medium. In the following emails, sent a few weeks apart, Kim expressed how well things were going.

April 8, 2020

"I just wanted you to know that even during all of this new normal event that's taking place in all of our lives, we are pushing forward as a team and I was able to close six cases last week! I saw seven new exams on Friday. I have six more scheduled this Friday, and five more scheduled on Monday. Patients are enjoying the virtual setting and the response has been remarkable. I am doing the contracts and consents right over the phone! And parents are just fine with that to get the ball rolling! The new patient calls are still coming in. I just booked a dad and a son at the same time for Invisalign! It's all in how you keep with the flow and the times and the ability to adapt. Thank you for what you have provided me as a treatment coordinator! They (virtual exams) actually are very easy! I see us continuing to do this past all of this mess!"

April 30, 2020

"There is no comfort zone anymore! I also wanted to let you know that I hit my goal and went OVER it for this month doing EVERYTHING VIRTUAL! My goal was at least 20 full case starts with signed contracts by April 30. I did 26 full and one express! The excitement I have of doing a combination of both exams is just wow! I did all of the contracts as well and collected. We had CASH FLOW!!! I did not think that was going to happen."

I was thrilled that Dr. Lupi and his team had found a way to stave off the shutdown with minimal damage. Even now that businesses have reopened, Dr. Lupi and his team continue to embrace the power of virtual exams.

Maybe you can relate. Maybe you saw the need to go virtual with your appointments during the shutdown. Countless business owners used this opportunity with varying degrees of success. About a month after the shutdown started, I hosted a Virtual 101 workshop and many people took that knowledge and ran with it, literally bringing in tens of thousands of dollars of production that would have been lost had they simply waited around.

What happened next is what I am most concerned about and one of the reasons I am writing this book. Many of those who jumped in and used the medium to survive in their business saw it as a temporary fix and quickly turned back to what they were comfortable with. I get it. Most offices became remarkably busy, even overloaded with clients who wanted and needed to get in. However, in the midst of the overwhelm, they also turned away from a potentially massive opportunity and an exciting future for their business and their patients.

My hope is that as you read this book, you will recognize that moment in time for what it was—a powerful chance to evolve and grow your business in ways that were not obvious until now. I want you to incorporate virtual fully into your practice, primarily for the business opportunity and secondarily because you never know when the world might stop again. As I sit in my office writing this section of the book, parts of Europe have just announced they will be closing down again. Governments are watching carefully with the threat of more shutdowns to come.

The Red Pill or the Blue Pill

In the dystopian movie *The Matrix*, a professional hacker called Neo is offered the choice between a red pill and a blue pill by rebel leader Morpheus. The red pill would take him to an uncertain future—one that would free him from what he was familiar with, allow him to see a new world of possibilities, and expand his understanding of what he was capable of. However, living in this new reality would be harsher, more difficult, and force him to unbelieve what he had believed up till now.

On the other hand, the blue pill would return him to the world he had always known. This world was comfortable and easy, though it would not lead him to the enlightenment he sought. Taking the blue pill would mean blissful ignorance, living in confined comfort without want or fear within the simulated reality of the Matrix.

When it comes to your future and the scalability of your business, I believe the shutdown was an opportunity to focus on a virtual component. Those weeks gave you a glimpse of living in the red pill world. In my humble opinion, it happened in part so you could visualize another pathway to grow your business. Like the red pill, going virtual requires you to leave the comfortable reality and jump in on the new possibility.

The blue pill world had you believing you had very few options, and most of them included you either working harder or giving up more. In the new red pill world, you can expand your reach, increase your revenue and grow *without* sacrificing more. The new red pill opportunity is scalability at a level unimaginable before.

VIRTUAL REALITY

Throughout the book you will see an occasional "Virtual Reality" box like this one. This is where I will give you some quick tips, hard hitting facts and other pointers that will serve to help you in your learning. Here is the first one.

Would you describe yourself as a person who would take the blue pill or the red pill? If you gravitate towards blue, keep reading. We're going to focus on skills that will increase your confidence and help you embrace the new. If you gravitate towards red, keep reading. You'll soon have a game plan to put into action.

As business owners, our job is to find as many ways as possible to scale our business. The ultimate achievement in scalability is a company that brings you income 24/7 and does not require you to be a part of the day-to-day tasks. Frankly, many people would be happy if they could simply accomplish even the latter.

When it comes to growing your practice revenue, you are bound by the fact that there is only one of you and only 24 hours in a day and 365 days in a year. You are an essential component to delivering your service. No matter how efficient your team is, it's impossible to automate what you do. So the options, up till now, have been limited.

Current Methods of Scale:

1. **Hire an Associate/Partner.** This typically involves a financial investment or giving up equity in the company. Although it hopefully duplicates your ability to serve patients, there is a cap on how often you can do it. When hiring an associate, you have to deal with the human aspect of sharing your business with another person. Not all associates work out and unless you find the right person, this method can cause major headaches.

2. **Buy a new building.** This may seem like it's a growth strategy, but it really is simply a matter of splitting your time. You have not duplicated your time; you have only made it easier for patients to fill it up.

3. **Work more hours.** This solution is the most obvious; however, working more is not the reason you got into your profession. This method has a natural limit because as you increase your work hours, you are decreasing the free time that you can make available.

4. **Add more products/Raise your fees.** This option requires that you be open enough to learn something new and have a bold enough marketing plan for the new products that they don't just sit on the shelf. Frankly, if you don't have a strong sales team to offer the main product you carry, then the likelihood of them being successful at selling additional products is probably extremely low.

   Raising your fees is something I am always a fan of. I actually think every professional reading this book should raise their fees by at least $500 tomorrow. I am serious. You do not charge enough for what you do. If you are worried about the market, then you need to focus on helping people see the value you provide. People buy based on value and convenience way more than they buy based on price. (I know many of you will not do this, but I felt I had to add it here because it is a viable way to grow your business.)

5. **Start a side business.** When you want to diversify your revenue stream without giving up on your original business, you start a side business. You might innovate a new software, a device to help in your current industry or a product completely outside of it. If your side business does well (and that is a big "if"), it can be the answer to your problem. However, the new business may gobble up significant startup resources before it can run on its own, and even if it does, you'll still be left with the scaling problem of the original practice.

Of course, this is *not* a comprehensive list and it's possible that you might see a few more ways to scale that I am not mentioning here. My goal is to lay out the challenge that you, as a business owner, face when it comes to scaling your income and the most common "answers" available to you up till now. None of these options are bad or wrong, I am simply pointing out that they tend to be suboptimal and often fall short of the freedom goal.

This is why I am passionate about using a virtual component in your business and 100% believe that if you use it properly, it can help you scale like never before.

VIRTUAL REALITY

Have you looked into any of these current methods of scale for yourself? How did it or would it affect your practice and your personal life?

For those of you who are on the fence about whether or not to embrace virtual business, I get it. Taking the red pill means you have to accept a new reality, one that might not be easy to digest at first, a new system involving a learning curve. You are going to have to be okay with getting out of your comfort zone. It will take time to implement, patience with your initial failures, and a different marketing plan in order to be successful.

Yet, when you do accept the challenge and see the new matrix, you can be confident that virtual has staying power, will create more freedom and help grow your business faster than you have previously imagined. As a matter of fact, while talking with one of my clients about the possible future, he mentioned one of the very real challenges some will face is not being able to handle the extra flow of business it can offer.

Virtual exams should be a new addition to what you offer sooner than later simply because it's the early adopters (those who make use of something new very quickly) who get the most gain in the market, while the early adaptors (Typically those who wait until after a concept or product has been proven) are left playing catch up.

So how can you use virtual exams and appointments to scale your business?

These are my top 5 compelling reasons why I believe now is the time to scale with virtual.

Reasons to Scale with Virtual

1. **Maximize your off hours and make money while you play**

    Imagine walking into your office on a Monday after spending the weekend on the beach. You look at your schedule and you notice there are five new clients who were not there when you left last week. That is because while you were off hanging out with your friends, sipping on something cool next to the waves, not having a single thought about your business. You had a Virtual Client Acquisition Specialist holding consults, closing deals and collecting money for you.

    Virtual business systems are not tied to office hours. You can leverage evenings, weekends, and even lunch breaks when you use virtual processes because a remote sales staff has increased availability. As a business owner, the goal is to make money while you sleep, and having automated systems and a virtual team can help you do just that. You will be able to draw in a clientele that is interested in the convenience of working with you at times that work for them — evenings and weekends.

2. **Maximize your schedule**

    Adding a virtual component to your business helps maximize the time you have. As you go online with your intake processes, sales quotes, and any other interactions that don't require you to be in-person, you free yourself up to do what you do best. Technology can automate the housekeeping tasks and give you your time back. This allows you to have less "chair" time and costs. Most practices report back that their consult time reduces by an average of 50% with virtual.

    Imagine being able to add one or more columns to your schedule. The ability to hold virtual appointments that can run simultaneously with your "live" appointments multiples you. You can essentially double, triple or quadruple the productivity of your office.

Warning! It's important to note that you may not be ready for the onslaught of new patients. You might not have the chairs available or the appropriate number of team members to be able to handle the increased volume. However, if you pace yourself, you can grow at 5-10 times the pace you have been used to.

3. **Offer a unique, valuable service**

Diversifying your business capabilities to include virtual gives potential clients more options. It allows people to choose to work with you remotely or in person, and for many of the rising generation, remote is the better option. Allowing for virtual sales means you value the client's time, you value their convenience, and you are willing to give them more options. It's also a differentiator in your area when it comes to competition. Above all else, people value time and convenience. If you can give those things to a patient who is deciding between you and the "other guy," you will win more often than not. When you offer the amazing benefits of virtual exams to a potential client and position it as a luxury service to them, you will have no competition to the right client.

4. **Flexibility of a remote sales team**

When you open the door for remote sales opportunities, your hiring pool for your sales team is limitless. You are no longer confined to a team that works within commuting distance from you; instead, you can recruit talent from almost anywhere.

Remember that one treatment coordinator or sales person who you really liked? You trained him or her so well and they were a huge asset to your team? Then one day they came in and said their spouse was transferred and they had to move across the country? Remember how bummed you were?

Now you have the ability to keep them on your team remotely with a few simple adjustments. Because of the virtual opportunities available to you, you have options.

When a valuable team member decides to move to another community or stay home with the kids, you no longer have to cut ties and recruit and train someone new. You can keep the amazing talent you have, regardless of where they choose to live.

5. **Charge people to come in live**

Many industries have adopted the model that office time for consultations is offered for free. As more and more businesses convert to a virtual model, office time will become more valuable. As a business, you can offer virtual consultations to your clients, or, if they choose to be in-person, you can charge a fee for that valuable office time. Different people are going to be drawn to both virtual and in-person interactions, and many will pay you for the opportunity to meet face-to-face.

VIRTUAL REALITY

If you had a remote team that was not bound by geographical area, who would you hire? Who do you know outside your area who could make killer sales presentations or be amazing at customer service?

Advanced Probability of Hitting Your Goals

Recently I was on a call with a well-established doctor whose office is bringing in $2.2 million per year. He has a goal of hitting $3 million during the upcoming year and the average treatment he offers is about $6,000. As we were talking, I quickly scratched out some numbers. According to my calculations, he would only need to increase his monthly case acceptance by about 12-14 new patients per month in order to hit his goal.

The challenge he was running into was his available days in the office. This doctor was willing to work extra days during the week, but not thrilled about it. I pointed out that if he established an invisible treatment coordinator who was running an invisible exam column either during his weekly schedule or on his days off to serve the people in his area who neither had the time nor desire to come in during regular hours, they could easily help him get those 12 extra starts per month and he could hit his goal in the next 12 months.

If you want to hit bigger goals and take a quantum leap in your finances, there is nothing that can help you do this faster than adding a virtual component to your offerings. After that introduction to this book, if you are not convinced to at least dive deeper into the power that virtual exams can bring to your business, then you should probably stop reading right now. Seriously. I won't be offended.

However, if you see the light, then I have a ton more to share with you. When you finish this book you will not only have a great sense of how you can establish virtual exams in your office, but the systems and practices will also help you in your traditional exam process. Everything in this book is designed to help you succeed.

VIRTUAL REALITY

A simple fact in many of our lives is we all have great intentions but often lack the time or ability to execute on them. Even as the high performer that you are, there are many things you want, intend and hope to do, but never get around to doing it. Just look at the list of books on your "to read" list or stacked up on the shelf.

If the last 10 pages have you already feeling overwhelmed, I may have a solution for you. In order to help you scale your business and use the full force of virtual exams in your business, I have developed a new service, dare I say category, in the orthodontic industry when it comes to new patient acquisition. We call it **My Virtual Start**. We have developed a system that allows you to have an invisible army of treatment coordinators to represent you as they hold virtual exams, close treatment, execute contracts and collect fees for you. If adding something like this to your practice in order to scale faster and close more clients while you are not in the office sounds interesting, go to www.MyVirtualStart.com to find out more.

The fact is none of us know what is going to happen in the future. If I would have told you in 2019 that there would be a time that you would no longer be able to do business in-person, it would have been a hypothetical scenario. We are now a little wiser and understand what is possible. Virtual is a tool that can make you more nimble and be able to continue to serve more people. It can help you feel more peace and prosperity, avoiding overwhelm and frustration because of the options it affords. If you are looking to scale your business, there has never been a better time to embrace virtual.

The principles taught in this book are not a sure recipe for success. There is no magic equation where if you perform these functions then you will get this result. There is no guarantee that if you incorporate any or all of my suggestions into your business that you will achieve certain levels of success. Be informed and make sure you are following your state and national legal standards. I cannot guarantee success, but I can promise you that you will become more resilient as you learn what works and what doesn't inside your unique business environment.

I hope I have created an intriguing enough argument for you to keep reading. Before we get to the meat of mastering virtual exams, let me share with you a lesson I learned while trying to learn how to surf that I believe relates to the opportunity before you now.

A few years ago I took surfing lessons in Maui. My instructor told me that when someone is learning to surf, they often wait for the wave to be underneath them before they start paddling. Even if they paddle as fast as they can to catch up to the wave, it is almost always too late.

An experienced surfer knows that to catch a wave, you have to start paddling before the wave is underneath you. Opportunities in life work the same way. When a wave of opportunity is headed your way, you have to start preparing before it gets to you if you want to ride it. Well, the next wave of opportunity is coming, and it's a big one.

Now is the time to upgrade your knowledge and skills. Now is the time to get familiar with virtual practices and embrace a new way of doing business. Now is the time to learn to reach more people and ultimately do more good. Welcome to Mastering Virtual Exams.

Challenge #1: Scaling Self-Assessment

Before we dive into your challenge, I want to share something with you about human beings and our retention abilities. Studies show that when you learn something new, you must practice it or teach it in the next two days. Otherwise, you become victim to the forgetting curve and lose about 75% of what you learned.

Big business knows this and they are always seeking out ways to help their employees retain expensive training. We're forgetful creatures and can lose even impactful experiences very quickly if we don't act on them right away. The more our brains touch on a subject, the more likely we are to remember it in the long-term. Throughout this book I'm going to give you challenges, and you'll want to complete them right away to retain the skills you are learning.

Even if you don't feel like it or you think it's silly, do it anyway! Remember that comfort is the killer to all progress. Being uncomfortable means that you are progressing. If you didn't want more than you have now, you wouldn't be reading this book. If you implement just one of these skills and put it into place in your office, your return on investment is going to be insane.

For this challenge you'll want to grab paper and pen for an old-school writing exercise. No, really, go get some paper and something to write with. The action of using your hands to form words on the page is another trick to stimulating creativity and retention. So now that you have your paper and pen, take some time to think about your unique business model and answer the following questions.

1. Write down three of your limiting beliefs about scaling your business. These are going to be false beliefs that are preventing you from pursuing your growth goals.

2. For each of these false beliefs, take some time to dig deeper. How long have I held on to this belief? Where did this belief originate? How have things changed for me since then? Does it make sense for me to hold onto this belief or let it go? Be sure to be kind to yourself. Just observe what has been taking place in your mind and reflect on whether now is the time to make a change.

3. If you could replace those three limiting beliefs with different ones, what would your new beliefs be? Take your time to craft these new beliefs, then post them by your bed or on your bathroom mirror.

Expert Interview: Real World Virtual Exams with Dr. Dan Bills

Dr. Dan Bills eased into the virtual medium slowly, starting with online marketing in 2018. His New Jersey orthodontic practice was thriving when he decided to work with a marketing group to capture more leads online. Together they developed software to attract local clients who were researching orthodontics on the web, not because of a shortage of new starts, but because Bills recognized that his target demographic was changing.

"The 50-year-old soccer mom was in my wheelhouse," Bills recalled. "It's the 20-something who doesn't really want to be there that was the challenge." The generation of parents who wanted to come in and be wowed by the office and the stellar orthodontic team was aging out, replaced by a group with entirely different priorities.

"As providers, we look at it as an hour-long consultation," Bills explained. "They see 15-30 minutes in the car, the time spent in the waiting room being around people they don't want to be around, then the hour-long consultation, followed by a return trip home. The appointment becomes a three-hour ordeal and they aren't going to invest that kind of time. They just want to do it online, and we want to give them that."

From that initial dabble into online marketing, Innovative Orthodontics lived up to its name. Bills fell in love with automating the process and had a solid lead-generating system in place by 2019. He would capture vital information and qualify candidates remotely before his clients ever set foot in the office, and it was working. He was even asked by the American Association of Orthodontics to lecture on *Virtual Consults as a Marketing Tool* in their May 2020 session. Then COVID hit.

"All of the sudden this happened, and I sat there and literally cried," Bills recalls. He watched with uncertainty as businesses and schools locked their doors and humanity cloistered in their homes. "Then, I gut-checked. I remembered we had this virtual system in place and that we could modify it to meet the need."

Bills got busy, working with his marketing group to create software that would work for virtual visits. Now Bills does just about everything possible virtually. He uses a full-team approach, with the TCs reaching out online, the doctors asking for reports and pictures, and the clinical team following up with the next steps like mailing aligners or making essential appointments. Slowly his team created a system that could work, even during a pandemic shutdown.

"I thought I had pieced together a 9-week band aid," Bills explained. "Then we got lots of positive feedback, and I realized I could do this after COVID." As Innovative Orthodontics changed their approach to virtual, the positive community response was decisive. All of a sudden his practice was bursting at the seams with too many appointments to easily manage.

The transition to virtual has made a meaningful difference in the time Bills spends in the office. Though he loves to work with his patients, he also desires to spend as much time as possible at home with his wife and daughter. Virtual technology allows him to do this. For example, Bills has an observation program with 1200 patients who require monitoring every six months. If he schedules every other one of those appointments virtually instead of in-person, he has eliminated 1200 appointments a year. His practice de-bonds around 1000 patients annually and has shifted the retainer check to virtual, eliminating those 1000 appointments as well. This reduction in in-office hours has had a significant impact for the entire team.

Bills suggests that orthodontists explore how virtual can enhance their own business models. "Consider the evolution of your practice with something that completely separates you from the competition. Last year I was lecturing about screen sharing and introducing Zoom to people. Now, my grandma knows how to use it. It's not awkward anymore."

2

Beginning with the end in mind

"To begin with the end in mind means to start with a clear understanding of your destination. It means to know where you're going so that you better understand where you are now and so that the steps you take are always in the right direction."

-Stephen R. Covey

In his classic work *The 7 Habits of Highly Effective People*, Stephen R. Covey guides his readers through a meditation. He asks his audience to imagine they are attending a funeral, and when they walk up to the casket, they discover the funeral they are attending is their own. He asks the reader to imagine in detail who will be speaking and what will be remembered. What sort of legacy will the reader leave behind?

For our purposes, beginning with the end in mind will not be so morbid. As we are focusing not on life, but on our virtual sales skill set, the end is the close. What does your close look like? Understanding what is happening during the close will shape the way you do everything else along the way.

If you want to increase your successful closing rates, the most important question to answer is, "Why are people saying 'No' to me?" Knowing the answer to this question is going to be more valuable than knowing why your clients are saying 'Yes.' It's nice to know why people want to do business with you, but knowing why they don't is imperative. A 'No' answer is an opportunity for you to improve. A 'No' means there is room for growth.

There are only three reasons why clients are saying 'No' to you.

3 Reasons Why People Say 'No' to You

A few years ago I was on a sales call with a potential client. I felt that I had discovered all the ways the doctor needed help, so I went in for the close. I was assuming the sale (which we will talk about later) and suggested that what he wanted and what I could do aligned. I offered to get him signed up for my program, explained the investment to him and then paused.

Suddenly, even though he showed no clues before, he started to hesitate. I could hear his excuse machine starting to whirl in his head. Sure enough, he brought up the first objection, "Well, let me think about it. I'll need to talk to my wife. I'll need to make sure it's in the budget."

Actually, that is three objections. However, it didn't matter to me. This was not my first pony ride, if you will. I knew that when someone throws out multiple objections, usually ones that are seemingly hard to argue with, he is not really giving me his true objection. These excuses are simply a way to cover up what is really going on. When this happens, the only option I have is to ignore their excuses and ask one specific question to get to the truth.

"Would you be opposed to me sharing with you something I have found about all my clients when they struggle with making a commitment and starting the program with me?"

"Of course not," he replied.

"I have found that most people hesitate for one of three reasons. They either don't trust me, they don't trust themselves, or they really don't want to make a decision either way. Which one of those three do you think it is for you?"

With that, I paused. There was silence on his end.

"That is a good question," he replied, then paused before he continued. "I would have to say, I don't really trust myself. I know I just got done telling you that I want to be successful, but I am not sure I will commit the time necessary to make this program a success. I really believe you can help me, so it's not you. I have tried so many other programs and consultants in the past and I just don't feel like I have been the best client. I am worried about my ability to actually do it and convince my team that I am serious this time."

Whoa! That was a lot of information, and none of it had to do with his wife, his budget or needing to think about it. But all of it was gold. Gold, because it helped me know what was actually going on and not believe the "default" answers he had given only a few moments ago. Unless I had asked that specific question, I would have never known the real issue. Even worse, if I would have done what "typical" sales training teaches and tried to overcome his originally stated objections, I would have been focusing on things that really didn't matter. I would have spent my time talking about things that were not his biggest concern. I would have likely lost that client.

A great mentor of mine taught me a truth years ago and it has never let me down. All objections can be compartmentalized into three specific areas. This means that there are only three reasons people say no to you.

- They don't trust themselves
- They don't trust you
- They don't want to decide

That's it. There really are just three reasons people say 'No.' If you can get them to tell you which specific one it is, you have a much higher chance of getting them to a 'Yes.'

To be fair, there are five major categories of objections that you will hear, but they will always fall into one of those three reasons. We will discuss those five later in order for you to identify where they belong. And when you learn to determine which category each of your prospect's excuses fall into, you can get really good at moving them past the 'No' answer.

Because of the written format of this book, I will be sharing my sales conversations as a script. However, I recommend you practice using key phrases you can bring into your natural conversation instead of rehearsing a full script. While scripts provide an important place to start, it's even more important to know how to go off book. You'll want to have a natural flow to your sales conversation and the script should be a template to show you where to go next. As you roleplay your sales conversations, you will find what feels best for you without leaning on a word-for-word script. You may prefer a bullet point list over a script because it allows you the flexibility to get through the points while still sounding authentic.

> **BONUS**: I am a visual and auditory learner so I wanted to add some bonus material for you via video training. Throughout this book you will have opportunities to watch video clips in order to help you experience the tone of how to say things, the body language cues to look for, and systems that can help you implement them more quickly. Go to https://dinowatt.com/mve-bonus/.

In his awesome book, *Never Split the Difference*, former FBI hostage negotiator Chris Voss explains that giving someone the opportunity to say 'No' to you gives them psychological freedom. In their mind, they feel more powerful than when they say 'Yes,' which feels more like a commitment. One they might not be ready to make yet.

The following conversation will help you understand how to get to the root of any 'No' answer. Any time someone says 'No' to you, regardless of the objection they might bring up, you're going to ask this question:

"Mrs. Davis, would you be opposed to me sharing something I've learned about myself when I'm thinking of not purchasing something?"

Of course, the client is going to say 'No' to this question. It's intentionally phrased this way because you want them to give you a 'No' answer. If you can get them to use the word 'No' while they are actually giving permission, it does something psychologically. It disempowers the word 'No' so it is no longer a conversation killer. You'll want to phrase the question this way on purpose to get that 'No' out of the way.

Here's how you'll continue:

"I find that there are only three reasons that I say 'No' to someone. Either I don't trust myself, I don't trust them, or I don't really want to invest in the product either way. Of those three options, which one best fits you?"

You just go ahead and put it out there to see how they respond. It's a sure way to get to the root of what is holding them back.

I know some of you might be wondering if you could ever ask that question during your close, and most likely, many of you won't. Not because it's difficult, but it's because you are not willing to take this and examples like it out of the book and actually practice saying it via role plays.

There is no need to shy from asking it at all. It's just a clarifying question. It's not insulting. It's not rude. It's simply a way to help people give you more information that you can use in order to help them not miss out on the opportunity to purchase from you.

In the half a dozen years that I have consistently asked this question, I have never once had a prospect feel that the question was rude and shut the conversation down. Rather, like in the example at the beginning of this chapter, this question gives them space to consider how they really feel. They understand that I sincerely want to know why they are not moving forward. More often than not, they will give you a very clear and more thought-out answer.

When you incorporate it into your sales presentation, it really is magical. You'll know how to handle each type of objection according to this answer. You'll know if they don't trust themselves, if they don't trust you, or if they don't really want to decide at all.

The three main objections are listed according to their frequency. Most often you will find that your prospects don't really trust themselves. Next you will find prospects who don't trust you. People who don't really want to commit either way are relatively rare, but I'll show you how to handle them, too.

People who don't trust themselves. These clients are not sure whether or not they can fulfill their end of the contract. They may not think they will be able to make the payments or complete the course. Or they don't trust their own buying decision ability. Maybe a past indulgence that turned out badly. These types of objections are the most common ones you will come across. The category includes objections like not having enough money, needing buy-in from a spouse, or that it's not the right time.

The "I have to ask my spouse" objection typically comes from a lack of trust from their spouse to let them decide on their own, probably because they have made a poor financial mistake before. When there is a purchase that needs to be made for the family and yet only one of the spouses is attending the meeting, it is highly unlikely that they never discussed the purchase ahead of time. (With the ability to search the internet and crowd source pricing, it's also unlikely that the potential client and their spouse do not have at least a general idea of how much the product investment is ... but I digress.)

This is why I suggest that you do everything you can to get both parties to be at the presentation. Even if they can't be physically there, they can be included via the phone or Zoom. However, your team needs to do more than just make this suggestion when they schedule the appointment. Make it a standard if at all possible.

Though it is important to know how to handle people who don't trust themselves, many of these objections can be handled during the screening process before you are ever in front of the client. If you do a good enough job in advance with your intake process, you will have already sorted most of these objections out.

People who don't trust you. These people don't feel that you can give them what they want. They are not yet convinced that you can deliver. It usually means that you have not done a good enough job letting them know what you know.

It can be difficult to hear that someone does not trust you. I understand that completely; I have had people say to me, "I don't believe you can deliver what you say you can deliver." But knowing about this concern is only going to help you. It will provide you with understanding so you can speak to what their concern is.

There is an essential communication flaw that becomes a huge problem with selling. When we are pitching, we often focus on listening to respond rather than listening to understand. We get so focused on getting through the presentation that we don't take the time to really listen. Just consider the last time you had a sales conversation. Maybe you were busy or are behind schedule. Maybe you tried to cram an hour and a half appointment into an hour and fifteen, not because you're efficient, but because you were trying to get through it. Have you ever been in the middle of a presentation and you find yourself redirecting the conversation to move quickly through it? It might be subtle, but the client can feel this redirection. They will likely feel that they are just one more thing you must get through.

If you really want to earn your potential clients' trust, you must be willing to listen to understand instead of listening to respond.

I have sat in on many presentations where I could see how the direction of the conversation would have changed dramatically if only the salesperson would have slowed down and taken a moment to really be there with the person. All people really only want three things when you are having a conversation with them. They want to know that you see them, you hear them and what they say matters. There is an old saying: *People buy from people they know, like and trust.* However, the more powerful way to look at it is: People buy from people they know like and trust … *them.* If you can help your potential clients feel this connection, you can throw out the formulated presentation and they will still want to buy from you.

People who don't want to make a decision. These people are time wasters. They are eternal shoppers who don't want to commit.

Let's see what these people might look like for an orthodontist. The potentials who don't really want to decide might not believe that braces are necessary. It could be a parent who believes that their child's teeth will eventually grow into their mouth. These people might want you to convince them that they need the treatment.

Another way people who don't want to decide reveal themselves is through making massive demands. These people want to see who will bend to their wants. I'm guessing you have experienced those clients before, and this next part will help you know how to handle them in the future.

First, let's get something straight: You are not in the business of convincing people to get what you have.

If you feel you have to continually convince people throughout the day, you are doing it wrong. If you ever feel burnt out and overwhelmed after a day in the office, this is a likely culprit. You are not in the business of convincing people to get what you have! People actually love to be sold, they hate to be pressured and when you go into convincing mode, you are going into pressure mode. You are in the business of giving people an opportunity and letting them take it or not.

And 'No' is a perfectly acceptable answer. Please don't get caught up in the idea that a person saying 'Yes' to you makes your treatment any better. It doesn't. And a 'No' doesn't make your treatment any worse. We need to divorce a potential client's response from the excellence of our business. You are striving to be the best in the business and you invite other people to take part in that. They get to make that choice to participate in what you are offering. It's as simple as that.

You may have heard the saying that the customer has the money and so they have the power, but that has not been my experience. You are offering an opportunity, an exchange, and if they say 'No' they are just opening up space for someone else who is interested in what you are offering.

In the book *No: The Only Negotiation System You Need for Work or Home* by Jim Camp, Jim warns about the danger of being attached to the outcome of a negotiation. When you are desperate for someone to do what you want them to do, they can smell it. That smell is repellant and it ultimately pushes them away and frustrates you.

Unattachment to the sales outcome is an important mindset that every member of your team needs to be familiar with. It can be a complete paradigm shift. It takes a huge mental load off and allows you to let go of potential clients who are not really a fit for your business. You can let them go their own way and know that you are still maintaining excellence in your industry.

VIRTUAL REALITY

Boldly asking your clients why they are saying 'no' to you takes both courage and practice. If connecting with people on a deeper level makes you feel uncomfortable, take a moment to consider why you feel that way. What might be keeping your relationships at a superficial level?

Sample framework to get past the most common objection (I don't trust myself)

TIP: Be sure to really pay attention to everything in these examples. There is so much I am doing with my words and my presentation that helps get the client to 'Yes' that I am not specifically talking about yet. Hopefully, by the end of this book your eye will be trained to spot all of them.

To watch the full training on the following script, go to https://dinowatt.com/mve-bonus/.

Dino: Congratulations! Dr. Tim says that you are a great candidate and in just 24 months, we can give you that full straight smile that you've been talking about. You can have the smile you always wanted.

Hannah: Yes! Fun. Interesting.

Dino: Yeah, I'm really excited about that. And Invisalign is a great choice. Hannah, would you be opposed if I actually went over some of the financial obligations right now?

Hannah: No, I wouldn't be opposed.

Dino: Okay, great. So I know that you spoke to Julie on the phone earlier, and she mentioned that you had asked about pricing, so she had given you a range of anywhere between $5,000 and $8,000. Do you remember that? Yes. Okay, cool. Well, the really good thing is that with your treatment we're going to be able to do everything, all of your retainers, your appointments and everything you need to make sure you get that smile will actually be only $6,300. However, with your insurance company you also get a $1,000 benefit. So your total that you are obligated for is only $5,300.

Hannah: Okay, that's not too terrible.

Dino: Yeah, I think it's actually a really great price. And I'm so glad we can give that to you. Can I ask you how much were you planning on putting down for a down payment? Or were you thinking about paying for the whole thing all up front?

Hannah: I actually don't think I'm going to put down a down payment at the moment. I need to figure out financially if I can afford this.

Dino: You need to figure out financially if you can afford it?

Hannah: Yeah. I mean, I'm a college student. I don't have lots of funds right now and paying for school and groceries and housing is kind of the most important at the moment.

Dino: Oh, I totally agree with you. That is really important to make sure you have those things paid. And I remember when I was a college student - funds weren't just flowing in, right? Exactly. I totally understand that. Can I ask a clarifying question? Is that okay? Sure. So one of the things that I found with people who've taken the opportunity to come here and have this exam together and go through all the conversation that we have, that when they are struggling to move forward with treatment it usually boils down to one of three things. Either they have a hard time trusting us, they have a hard time trusting themselves, or they don't want to make a decision either way. Can you help me understand which one of those three might you be?

Hannah: Probably just, honestly, myself. I just don't know if I can financially afford this and put down the down payment and the monthly payments.

Dino: Okay, awesome. Thank you for sharing that with me. Other than just the payment and the monthly fee, is there any other concern that you might have?

Hannah: Honestly, that's pretty much the major one, the only one I'm really concerned about.

Dino: Okay, cool. Very good. I'm so glad to hear that you have faith in the treatment itself and you think that we can actually help deliver that. And also that you really are looking to move forward as long as you can make it make sense financially for you. So Hannah, let me ask you then if you were to put some money down, how much were you thinking about putting down?

Hannah: About $500? That's what I can afford at the moment.

Dino: Okay, awesome. Very good. So let me do the math real fast on here. So with $500 down, you would be actually looking at a payment of about $200 a month. The more you put down at the beginning, the smaller your payments are, and we love to work with people with their payments. So is that the best you can do with that down payment?

Hannah: Well, I might be getting some taxes back soon. I could probably do $750.

Dino: Okay, great. Just get that calculation. All right, because you're willing to put down that $750 and use your taxes for that, your new monthly payment is below the $200 mark. It's actually only $189. So I'm really glad that we can make that happen for you. And you know what is even better than that? We can get you in for a scan to get those Invisalign ordered and get them ready to go. Either Monday, June 1st or Tuesday the 2nd at 9am. Which one will work better for you?

Hannah: Tuesday would work better.

Dino: Okay, great. So do me a favor, Hannah. Will you go and check your email inbox right now? We sent you an email previously that we're going to need. I'm also going to send you a DocuSign for the agreement. Have you used DocuSign before? Yeah. Okay, great. So I'm also going to send you a link right now through the chat box right here. That link will take you directly to the agreement that I'm looking at right here on the screen. We're going to click on that.

- Did you notice how I led Hannah to give me a 'No' answer quite early in the conversation?

I allowed her to get that word out so that it was no longer acting as an impediment. It removes that energy from the throat and opens people back up to possibility.

- Did you see how I worked the which-type-of-No-are-you question right into the conversation?

You'll want to get really good at asking this question based on what is happening at the time. Most communication fails not because of the communication itself, but because the setup for the communication fails. If you do it sincerely and without judgement, people are going to open up to you.

Hannah wants to do this. She has been waiting her whole life for that confident smile, but her concern is with herself and her ability to make it happen. I simply got some clarifying information so I could walk her through that concern.

- Did you pinpoint where I asked Hannah to move forward with treatment?

If you look back, you'll notice that I never did. One big challenge most salespeople have is moving the sales process forward. Great salespeople ask a question, appreciate the answer, and then move forward. We'll focus more on this concept later on.

With Hannah, I learned that her objection was not with the treatment or what we could deliver. I knew if I could get the payment right, she would be good to go. So I proceeded to line things out for her and move the conversation forward.

- Did you see the conversation shift when I asked Hannah how much she could put towards a down payment?

Asking this question is key because I am allowing her to think about and then say out loud what she can do financially. There is an old sales adage: *He who names price first, loses.* If you tell people what you want first, you lose. The idea is for the client to name a price first and you can do this by asking them about a down payment.

Let's look at an example of naming the price in action. You have an amazing product and the minimum down payment is $500. If you are negotiating with a client and you tell her about your minimum first, you may never know that she had $2k saved up for your product. That's $2k in your bank account that you would have waited months to see if you had let her know your minimum first.

- Did you see how the conversation went straight into signing the contract and processing the down payment?

You'll want to be organized and have all these pieces in place in advance because when you get a payment from someone, they become committed. There is an energy that comes with exchanging money that is palpable. Sometimes when you order something online but you haven't paid for it yet, you might still decide against it. But once you pay for that item, you are much more committed. I want Hannah to show up to her appointment on Tuesday, so the deposit is important.

3 Overlooked sales tools you already have that can shift a sale

Now that we have shined a light on the sales close and the reasons why people are saying 'No,' let's switch gears and talk about some of the best sales tools for locking in a sale. These are tools that you already have but are probably overlooking. I don't see them used nearly often enough in business, so it's time to pull these tools off the shelf, dust them off and start using them to close more sales.

When I was twelve I got braces. It was right after the trauma of my parents' divorce. Have you ever heard someone reassure a child that it was not their fault the parents were fighting? Well, in my case, I was literally the reason my mom and dad fought every month. They would fight over who had to make the payment.

My mouth was jacked up! I had a supernumerary tooth that was twisting my front two teeth on top of each other and blocking the teeth on either side of them. In addition to my funky mouth and the stress of my parents divorce, I was also the shortest kid in class and, just for good measure, let's not forget that I had the name "Dino" in the 70's and 80's. Things were not going so well for little Dino.

But getting braces was the best thing ever. Prior to braces, there is not a single school picture or family photo where I would smile with my teeth showing. I would grin as big as possible, but I was not about to show those pearly whites. But then, I got braces.

I had braces for four years. That's right, I was a terrible patient for Dr. Frosh. I ate all the wrong things. Sometimes you think the patients aren't cooperating because they are not paying attention, but sometimes the patients are doing it because they are getting attention. That was me. I loved them. I would show off my brace-face as much as I could. It made me feel special. It gave me the positive attention I craved. It was back in the day when braces were much more invasive, and I even had full headgear. (Let's be clear, I wanted attention, but I wasn't crazy. I only wore the headgear at night). I had those braces on for four years, and it changed my life. I loved them.

Sales Tool #1 - Your story

The first tool that is often underestimated and incredibly underutilized in the sales process is your personal story. What is your story around this product or service? What is your client's story?

Stories connect us. From the time we are very young, we have been programmed to equivocate stories with love and connection. For many of us, one of our first sentences was around the idea of, "Tell me a story." It's been said that our brains are wired to pay attention when someone says, "Let me tell you a story." If you simply use the word 'story,' peoples' brains will light up, get engaged and begin to connect.

If you do not have a specific personal experience with the product or service, then use one that you experienced with either a family member, friend or even a previous client.

No matter your industry, you have a story you can tell. If you are in the travel industry, then tell the story about your favorite personal vacation story. In real estate? Talk about your first home or the disaster home you bought. Design computers? Tell them about how little you knew until your product came along. Sell Lasik eye surgery? Talk about how your spouse's life has been transformed by the ability to see again. Whatever the industry, the power of a story applies across any industry. Remember, stories connect us.

To make your story engaging, it should address these three specific questions:

1. Where did you (or the subject) start out? Include how you felt and what problem you were facing.
2. What happened when you got the product/service?
3. How has it positively affected you?

You'll want to get really good at asking your client to share their story, and then share yours. Even if your prospective client never went on vacations as a kid, she is still going to want to connect and tell you a story. She'll say she always wanted to travel with her family, but her parents couldn't afford it. She might recall that she heard all of the other kids in class talk about their family vacations and she always longed to be a part of that.

If you really think about it, you probably have more than one story you could tell. There is the time you went on your first vacation as a kid. Then the time you went all by yourself to a country where you didn't speak the language and then the time where you went with your first love. Having multiple stories to pull from will help you be able to find the one that you think will best connect to your potential client.

The social part of us that craves connection is going to wake up when we share our stories with each other. Listen to their story, and then share yours. You can use the power of story throughout your presentation, personalizing it to each prospect. If you ever find yourself in the middle of a presentation and you feel the need to move the discussion forward or redirect, use your story to get things back on track. You can weave your story throughout the presentation.

That story is way more powerful than what amenities a hotel has, or which travel insurance is going to be best. Stories sell more powerfully than anything else.

VIRTUAL REALITY

When did you realize your future was in orthodontics? Was it when you got your first dental impression, when you watched all the kids around you get braces, or maybe as a college kid trying to find the right career path?

Sales Tool #2 - What do they want?

This question is the most powerful question you can ask anyone, including yourself.

What do you want?

Getting to the true desire that is motivating your client is essential if you want to close the deal. You want to find out what your client loves. You want to find out what your client dislikes. You want to be able to pinpoint the reasons why that client is seeking you out. When you allow people to talk about what they want, they will sell themselves on your product.

I know you might be thinking that you have this one down. You may think you already know why your prospects are requesting a consultation. Well, let me give you some insights from the hundreds of offices I have visited. If you're in an orthodontic office, you'll likely have an intake form with a space for the referring dentist and a space for the medical concern. It'll say 'crowding' or 'overbite.' But let's get something straight — that medical concern on the intake form is *not* the reason your prospective client wants a consultation. There's always more to it than that.

In short: ***What they really want is NOT your product. It's what your product can do for them ... emotionally.***

Getting to the bottom of what each client really wants begins with the first phone contact. Your phone ninjas need to be well-trained and understand that their time on the phone with prospects is valuable. From this very first contact, we want that client to know that we are listening and want to know all of their concerns. Be inquisitive rather than accusational and allow people to open up to you.

Let me take you back to Hannah, the college student who was concerned about closing on braces because she wasn't certain if she trusted herself financially. When Hannah communicated her concern, I reiterated that concern and then I asked if there were any other concerns. I will not move forward in the sales conversation until I have allowed her to verbalize any issues she has. I will wait until she says she has no more concerns, and only then do we move on. We can use this same principle to come to an understanding of what the client wants.

Usually, the client's first answer is a surface-level answer. Don't simply write it down and move on. Remember, we are trying to understand the client's desires so we can be sure to address them. So I follow up with, "We want to make sure you get the best experience possible, so is there anything else you are concerned about?" Listen, write down their answer, and ask if there is anything else they want to add. Keep asking "What else?" until the client indicates that they have no other concerns. Don't worry, the client is not going to be annoyed by this because the number one subject people like to talk about is themselves. So take this chance to listen. You can have the one weird office that really listens to people.

Maybe the client is having a hard time sleeping at night. Maybe it's difficult to chew. Maybe their kid is getting bullied because of his teeth. Ask what they don't like about their smile. Ask why they haven't looked for a solution before now. Ask how their smile has affected their adolescence, their work, their relationships. Allow them to talk and guide them to see how their problem has cascaded into other areas of their life. The idea is not to stick a knife into their wound, but to help them unpack what their problem is really costing them.

Helping people with these types of deep desires is the heart of your business. You are not in the business of straightening teeth. You are in the business of serving others and making their lives better. That's where the focus should be. Knowing these motivating desires in each of your clients does not make you superficial or manipulative. It makes you the best at what you do.

People buy what they want, not what they need.

I'll say it again. People do not by most things they actually need, they buy what they want. No one *needs* a 55-inch television or to eat at McDonalds. They *want* to. They buy emotionally first and then back it up with logic. Most salespeople show people what they need instead of talking about what they want. Talk about what they want - connect it to their emotional why, and then get busy and deliver what they need.

Sales Tool #3 - Assume the sale. The. Entire. Time.

When you have a prospective client, when is it agreed that the sale is going to go forward? That sale is going forward from the moment that client calls to make the consultation. At least it is in my mind, and it should be in yours as well.

If you have a client asking for your time, you should assume that they are going to close with you. The expectation is that they are going to buy the product, enroll in the course or purchase the training. As a salesperson, you've got to have the mindset that things are always moving forward. Too often we get on autopilot and go through the mental presentation checkpoints in our head. "Ok, I got through the welcoming part, now on to the next part."

Then when we get to the end of the checkpoints, the buildup in our head of accomplishment is so big and we don't want it all to be for not, so we get hung up on asking for the sale. Some people feel their chest tightening up. Some people get sweaty. Some people avoid the close by starting a distracting conversation. Some take a deep breath and mentally brace themselves for the discomfort of asking a prospective client to agree to the very reason they walked into the room or got on the call. The challenge with most people is that asking for money is the weirdest part of the process.

It makes sense. Asking a virtual stranger that you met just moments ago to give you money, generally speaking, is weird. Money is an emotional topic and for many people it's not something they are comfortable talking about anyway. Now you are going to ask them to give you theirs? In my live training, I often talk about the psychology of money and how it's important for the salesperson to get clear with their money issues because whatever their energy is around it comes through in the presentation.

What do some money issues look like?

-   Backing off as soon as someone offers an objection
-   Not aggressively following up after the prospect leaves
-   Apologizing for the price of the product or service
-   Finding ways to make the price lower through made up discounts instead of building the value

All of the above are simple signs that you might not be comfortable with talking about money in general, let alone asking for it. That is a problem when your entire business revolves around asking people to give you theirs.

It's important to clarify that "assuming the sale" does not mean avoiding the sale or the investment.

VIRTUAL REALITY

Making the mental shift to assuming the sale takes active practice. When your thoughts begin to question the sale, steer them back over to assuming the sale territory. In time this will be the natural path of your thought.

I was recently in an office where the sales team was actually trained not only to avoid asking for the sale, but to avoid sharing the price of the treatment all together. They would play this weird game of only telling people the expected down payment and the monthly payment. This, I was informed later when questioning the tactic, was intended to get the prospect to only focus on the smaller number rather than the big number.

Most salespeople try to avoid coming across as shady or sneaky, but this strategy seems to embrace it. Not only do I think this is a questionable tactic, but when I asked if most people ask for the total investment anyway, they replied, "Well, yeah, but that's how I was trained."

Suffice it to say, I do not recommend this approach. That is not to assume it doesn't work and if the data shows that it's been effective, then maybe there is a case to be made. Personally, I don't see the need for it. If you don't feel the value of the service you provide is justified by the investment you are asking for, then change the price. However, if you like the number you are asking for, then your job is to create an overwhelmingly obvious value that your clients will feel happy to invest in.

There is psychology that happens on the other side of the table as well. The prospect often experiences the desperate, almost irrational need to know the price of the thing they came there to get.

In the dynamic that happens in the sales process, something interesting happens. You, the gatekeeper of the product, need to build your case as to why the prospective client will benefit from your product. The prospect wants to make sure you can deliver the product but is typically distracted by the most uninteresting thing about it: the price.

Potential buyers will do almost anything to get you to name a price. From before they even call you or walk in the office, their mind is focused on getting to the bottom line, "How much does it cost?" The longer you hold this from them, the more insane they get. People will even act crazy if they can't get you to give them a price, sometimes even before they know all the benefits of the thing you are selling.

Often people will ask you for the price in the first few minutes. I know this can be challenging because you don't want to look like you are dodging the question, but you still need time to explain or justify the price tag. Whenever I get in a situation where someone asks me for a price before *I* am ready to give it, I simply reply with, "Well, the good news is, if we determine that I am not a fit for what you need, it will cost you nothing." It usually makes them smile and nod in agreement.

So, instead of trying to give you multiple tactics to become *zen* with the ability to ask for the sale, I am going to ask you to build up your assume-the-sale muscle. I want you to get to a place in your mind where if someone says 'No' to you, it's a shock to your system. I want you to develop a belief that every single person who comes to your office has already made up their mind to go with you and that your conversation is just a formality. You should be so convinced of this that hearing the words "We are going to pass" sounds like they are speaking a foreign language. That will only happen with practice and confidence in the product you offer.

In my previous conversation with Hannah, I never stopped the process to ask if we were good to keep going. I heard her objections and I addressed each one. I knew what the next step was, so I set the appointment.

The human brain likes flow and rhythm. The listener's thought process will continue in that flow until something stops it. Think about how annoying it is when you are cruising down a highway and then someone tries to merge into your lane by slowing down. What happens to your attitude? When only a second ago you were coasting along, singing your favorite 80's classic and then, because someone decided to slow down while merging, you are suddenly aware that there is a problem. All the warning bells in your head go off, saying, "Pay attention, watch out, be careful, don't trust that they see you!" When you stop the flow of the conversation by going to the "Ask for the Sale" moment, that happens to your prospective client.

As a salesperson, you are facilitating and allowing that flow. You must move forward as if this is all part of the assumed conversation. The price is a part of the flow, not a big deal that needs an extra breath and a gearing up for. Don't worry. Although the person is wanting to hear the price, you don't need to make the moment a big deal. This takes practice, but assuming the sale will always move you and your clients closer to your goals.

The key is to hold the belief that this person called you and then took time out of their own busy day to come in for an appointment. They want something you offer, so you proceed with the next step of sale. Assume the sale!

As you begin with the end in mind and watch for ways to improve your sales close, you'll absolutely look at your numbers. Those sales percentages are a great indicator and can show you holes in your approach and how you can better train your team.

But you also need to understand that a 'No' answer is okay. It opens up the opportunity for someone else to choose what you have to offer. When someone says 'Yes' to you, that does not make your service better. When they say 'No,' that does not make your service worse. You can have humility and still see your value.

If you create a culture that places your excitement, pride, and value on a 'Yes,' then you have to do the opposite with a 'No.'

You cannot have one without the other. However, if you detach these feelings from the sales close, it will make all the difference in your business. When you really feel that your office is excellent, that your team is amazing and that you are serving others and doing good, people are going to be drawn to you. They will feel that energy from you and will want to partner with you. Everybody wins.

Challenge #2: Go live with your story.

Think back to the beginning of this section. What do you remember about my braces story? Could you relate to it in any way? Did you feel like you got to know a little more about me? Did you feel I was building a relationship with you through my "human" experience?

That is the power of story and why you need to get in touch with and tell yours as often as possible to your clients. Whatever your industry, you most likely work in it because you have a story about it. Even if it's not your personal experience, you have stories you can tell that will connect with the person in front of you and build a stronger relationship.

So for this challenge, I want you to tell your story. This is your chance to really focus and get your story straight. If it's helpful to you, put pen to paper and write your story down first. Get clear on what motivated you when you were in your client's shoes. Depending on what you are selling, it may not be your personal story — it might be your kid's or your friend's or your grandma's — but you can still use it in your presentations. You'll want your story to be succinct but also a bit revealing as this is not a surface-level story, but a chance to connect with clients. You should be able to tell it in under three minutes. In the spirit of becoming more comfortable on-screen, you won't simply be telling the story either. You'll be going live to share your story on the social media platform of your choice.

You heard my braces story, now it's your turn. Get your story lined out, then go live and tell it. It is empowering to hear yourself tell your story on-screen. It may feel awkward to you at first and that's okay, it's part of the process. Just like everything else in life, this will get easier as you practice it more, whether the difficulty is getting in front of the camera or smoothing out any technical issues.

It's time to get used to seeing yourself on the screen. It's time to get out of your comfort zone and talk without waiting for a response. Whatever business you are in, whatever service or product you are selling, you are doing it for a reason. Rediscover your personal story and start connecting with others by sharing it.

Expert Interview: Real World Virtual Exams with Dr. Tom Marcel

Among the vineyards and hills of California lies Marcel Orthodontics, where Dr. Tom Marcel and his team have been rolling out virtual exams. Marcel tried different methods, made adjustments to his process, and made discoveries along the way about what worked best for him. Here are some of his best practical tips for creating a successful virtual orthodontic experience.

Marcel found that one of the simplest ways of directing his potential clients to virtual is to offer them the choice between a virtual or an in-office exam when they first call the office. This was one way to ease your team into the virtual exam experience and work out any bugs in the system before promoting online. He also installed the Smile Snap add-on to capture leads directly from his website and found that virtual exams follow organically from this marketing method. "Make it easy for the patient," Marcel recommends. "Having an easy way for them to get information is key."

His front-desk team reports that many new patients are thrilled that they don't have to come in for a consultation. Rather than having to manage getting time off of work or pulling their kid out of school or taking a long lunch hour, they get their time back through the virtual experience.

In the beginning, Marcel toyed with using a live app like Facetime for the virtual exams. However, he found that these synchronous exams were taking a lot of his time. Patients would inevitably ask a lot of questions during these live consults, Marcel wanted to provide great responses, and the time added up. He prefers instead to receive the smile pictures and send a quick text message in response. He usually texts something like: *I looked over your pictures and you are a great candidate for orthodontics. Christine will be in touch with you to talk about finances and get you scheduled. I look forward to meeting you!* This simple photo-and-text swap takes just a few minutes and eliminates time spent scheduling a live exam and dealing with client questions that will be addressed later in the process.

Marcel found that one great touch-point for his clients is to record and send a 30-second video introducing the patient to the practice. He keeps these videos simple and quick, personalizing them with the person's name, and letting them know how much they are going to love Marcel Orthodontics. The video is a way to connect personally without giving patients the opportunity to interrupt and ask questions. "Make sure you are presenting well. Dress appropriately and use good lighting," Marcel advises. "You don't want to be by the pool sipping a cold one."

Virtual patients are carefully tracked in Marcel Orthodontics' management system so the leads don't get lost. When one of these clients comes into the office for the first time, that fact is blasted on their chart so that every member of the team, from the front desk to the doctor, can give them first-rate introductory treatment. He and his team have been able to redistribute the workload with the help of virtual tools, with his clinician performing follow-up with retainers, his TC keeping track of growth and guidance, and Marcel handling the clients in liners. "Because sometimes the patients only need two or three liner checks from start to finish, I have felt that it's important for the doctor to have that touch-point with them," Marcel points out. "They value that."

When he first began holding virtual appointments, Marcel's enthusiasm was tempered with a healthy dose of scepticism. He thought if he could close half of the leads generated online, then the initiative would be a success. After tracking the sales cycle for these leads, he was surprised to discover that his office was closing virtual clients at a rate of 6:7, right on track with his in-office closing rates. His team has made an effort to answer the online requests in a timely manner until the workflow has become second nature to them, and his clients are responding and signing up. "The patients have the three pieces of information they want. They know they are a candidate, they know the timeframe, they know the price point," Marcel shares. "There's no reason for them to go hunting somewhere else, so they sign up."

3

Your sales personality and selling to theirs

Two friends drove past the city limits on a dirt road leading to open fields dotted with horses and orchards. Walter pulled the car to the side of the road and vividly described to his friend what he was going to build on this desolate land. He wanted to convince his friend Arthur to buy all the surrounding acreage.

Walter told Arthur, "I can handle the main project myself. It will take all my money, but I want you to have the first chance at this surrounding acreage. In the next five years, it will increase in value several times."

Arthur looked around and thought to himself, "Who in the world is going to drive twenty-five miles for this crazy project? His dream has gotten the best of his common sense." Arthur gave Walter all the excuses a good friend could give while trying not to squash the other's dream.

Even after Walter implored Arthur to buy the remaining land, Arthur refused to concede. Money was a little tight, he said, and now was not the best time to invest. But he would think about it and get back to Walter later.

"Later on will be too late," cautioned Walter. "You better move on it right now."

Art Linkletter failed to see the vision of his close friend Walt Disney. One year later, on July 17, 1955, Walt opened Disneyland and Art was the Master of Ceremonies. Linkletter had missed an opportunity of a lifetime by failing to purchase the land surrounding one of today's most well-known amusement parks: Disneyland.

While Arthur had failed to see the vision of his close friend, someone else hadn't. In 1954, the year Disney was building his dream, the Fujishige family purchased fifty-six acres of strawberry fields across the street for $2,500. In the late 1990s, the Disney Corporation paid the family just under $100 million for the land. Whose fault was it that Linkletter didn't see the opportunity? Was it Disney's—or Linkletter's?

This is how author Woody Woodward begins his book *D.R.I.V.E Sales: The Secrets to increasing sales by 400%*. And no, that is not a typo, 400% is correct. He also says, "You lose 80% of sales just by opening your mouth." That is a lot of loss. Let's change those odds for you.

Throughout this book you will learn many different ways to communicate better with your potential client. These pages include insights from reading body language to using words that sell that will help you start more patients and close more deals. However, if you do all that but you are not "speaking their language," then you will still be working harder than you need to.

Woody has been a friend for years and when he shared his book with me I was hooked. I read the entire book in less than 24 hours. While on a business trip. Between training. And working off only a few hours of sleep. That is how good it is and how much it spoke to me.

Interestingly enough, around the same time he asked me about the Selling Through the Screen Challenge I held. I gave him access to all of the recordings of that information and he consumed it as quickly as I did his book. We both saw an instant connection in what we are sharing with the world.

For me, one thing was clear: I had to add a mention of the DRIVE Sales system in this book so that you have an even higher chance of success in implementing the information in Mastering Virtual Exams. When I asked for his permission, Woody graciously told me to use as much of it as I wanted. The following pages in this chapter are almost directly from his book. I say "almost," because I have changed a few of the words and examples to be more precise for you in the private practice field.

To get an even deeper understanding, I highly recommend you go to Amazon and have a copy rushed to your door as soon as possible. For now, here is an in-depth look at why you need to learn this language.

D.R.I.V.E.

There is one reason why our pitches fall flat. We are not speaking our potential customer's buying language. The business graveyard is littered with the lost opportunities of individuals who could not convey their message to make a deal.

Consider the following:

- Nolan Bushnell, founder of Atari, was Steve Jobs' first boss. Jobs offered Bushnell one-third of Apple for $50,000. Bushnell was unconvinced and passed on the investment. Why?

- Billionaire Ross Perot could have owned a majority of Microsoft in 1979 for $60 million. But he never pulled the trigger. A majority of Microsoft today would be worth $512 billion—an 850,000 percent ROI. Why did he not see the value?

- Myspace CEO Chris DeWolfe was offered Facebook for $75 million by Mark Zuckerberg, but he passed. Why did DeWolfe not see the full potential of Facebook?

- In 1999, Excite could have bought Google for $750,000. Two years later, Excite filed for bankruptcy. What went wrong?
- Decca Records passed on the Beatles. The Beatles went on to become one of the biggest rock-and-roll bands in history. How did Decca miss that opportunity?
- Western Union was offered the telephone from inventor Alexander Graham Bell for $100,000 and passed. Why did they not see the potential?
- In 2006, Yahoo! shook hands with Mark Zuckerberg to purchase Facebook for $1 billion—and then backed out. What caused them to back out? In 2016, Verizon purchased a collapsing Yahoo! for $4.6 billion. And Facebook is now worth $538 billion.

There are five buying personalities that DRIVE sales: Directors, Relators, Intellectuals, Validators, and Executives. You pitch based on your own DRIVE, which means you do not effectively sell to the other eighty percent. The good news, though, is that the easiest sale you will ever make is to someone with the same DRIVE. Here is what you will learn through the DRIVE Sales System™:

- How to sell to each DRIVE, thus potentially increasing your sales by 400 percent
- How to capitalize on your own DRIVE to increase your revenue
- How to prepare your offer for maximum impact using DRIVE
- How to use a reassociation to create buying behavior
- How to close the sale with "ASK. Don't Tell."
- How to close the sale with "SHOW. Don't Tell."
- How to save the sale with PICKS

Before you get the keys to the sales kingdom and are set loose with these new techniques, you need to understand your personal DRIVE System—why you buy and what motivates you—so you can be prepared to craft the proper pitch to your potential customers. Once you do, you'll be able to dramatically increase your sales

The DRIVE Assessment

Ernő Rubik invented one of the most popular three-dimensional puzzles in history. His Rubik's Cube is undoubtedly one of the most well-known toys in the world, with over 350 million units sold. This simple three-inch cube has over forty-three quintillion combinations (43,252,003,274,489,856,000, to be precise). Despite its incredible complexity, it can be solved using seven key algorithms, or seven specific steps. In fact, in 2018, thirteen-year-old Yusheng Du set the world record for solving it in 3.47 seconds.

Just like the Rubik's Cube, every human personality has a myriad facets, moods, preferences, opinions, and habits. There is, however, a simple algorithm that explains why we buy and why we do what we do. It is called DRIVE. Rubik's three-inch cube has seven steps to solving the quintillion options, and your DRIVE consists of a mere seven characteristics that move your behavior.

Follow the two simple steps below to discover your DRIVE, and learn how to motivate and influence behavior in a way you have never experienced.

DRIVE Assessment Instructions:

Step 1. Read the seven words in Groups A through E.

D.R.I.V.E. Assessment	D	R
INSTRUCTIONS	Experiencing Life	Relationships
1. Read Each Card First	Life's Purpose	Influence
2. Rank The D.R.I.V.E. Cards based on the card with the most words that MAKES YOU FEEL IMPORTANT, not what is important to you.	Freedom	Service
	Creativity	Family
	Performing	Friends
3. Example: R, E, D, I, V	Overcoming	Parent
© 2020 - Wendy MacAsted	Appearance	Spirituality

I	V	E
Knowledge	Recognition	Winning
Learning	Accepted	Control
Health	Praise	Work
Nature	Trust	Goals
Moment	Respect	Security
Standards	Validation	Providing
Organized	Being Needed	Problem Solving

Step 2. Read through them again and choose the ONE group with the most words that make you feel important, not what is important to you. This is critical in properly identifying your DRIVE. There are things that are important to you, like work or family, but those items may not make you feel important. Choose the one group that makes you feel important. Rank the groups from one to five (#1 being the highest). If you get stuck between two groups, ask yourself, "Which one could I not live without?"

If you are struggling between two, then pick the one you feel is more "you" most of the time and then the other will be your secondary. They are usually complementary to each other. The thing to remember is none of these are better than the other, it's simply a matter of personal preference. However, what is important is that you understand how to hear all of them so that you can identify your clients DRIVE and speak their language.

Below is a more in depth look at each DRIVE. As you read check in with yourself to see if the descriptions validate the DRIVE you chose.

> ## VIRTUAL REALITY
>
> Did you easily determine which sales personality a friend or family member has? Often it's easier to pinpoint the personality of someone we know well than it is to understand our own. If you are stuck trying to figure out your DRIVE, as someone close to you which one they think you are.

DIRECTOR

A Director loves to feel free and independent, has a purpose for what they do, and thrives on experiencing life. They enjoy being creative and discovering new things. Directors are innovators, performers, orchestrators, and collaborators; they can take an immense amount of diverse information and synthesize it into information easily grasped by the masses. They are great in social settings and in bringing people together to make something happen. They find joy in overcoming obstacles and making a difference in the world.

Strengths

- Creative, outgoing, and passionate about what they do
- Spontaneous and adventurous in the way they approach life
- Expressive, fashionable, stylish, and confident
- Don't give up and are eternally optimistic
- Can be strong-willed and will not allow themselves to be pushed around
- Have a clear vision of what they want and are willing to sacrifice for that purpose
- Open-minded and think outside the box

Weaknesses

- Sometimes unsympathetic with those who complain
- Hard on themselves about their appearance
- Can be a non-team player and at times isolate
- Frustrated when people do not value their creativity
- Disappointed when they are not achieving their life's purpose
- Others cannot keep up with their impulsiveness and spontaneity
- Can get exhausted from always trying to do everything

Buying Motivators

Directors are motivated to create their ideal *Lifestyle*. When purchasing a product or service, they want to know how it is going to enhance their lifestyle or give them the life they want. They are attracted to products or services that will help them achieve financial freedom, time freedom, or give them a VIP experience.

Examples of Successful Directors

- Walt Disney (Disney)
- J. K. Rowling (Author – Harry Potter Series)
- Sara Blakely (Spanx)
- Theodore Geisel (Dr. Seuss)
- Elon Musk (Tesla, SpaceX)

RELATOR

Relators find value in building strong, healthy, long-term relationships. Relationships are both important to them and make them feel important. In the workforce, their strength is in networking and building other people up to a higher level of productivity and accountability. If their relationships are struggling, they feel challenged to be productive. Relators garner energy and security through their relationships. They are loyal to their friends, enjoy having the power of influence, strive to be good parents, and are service-minded. They desire to see their relationships continue to deepen and grow.

Strengths

- Compassionate, loving, and caring in relationships
- Charitable, forgiving, and a peacemaker
- Easy to talk to and a great listener
- Puts the team, family, or friends before their own needs
- Feels secure in their relationships
- Natural team leader
- Often will be the first to raise their hand to volunteer

Weaknesses

- Serves and sacrifices too much, often to their detriment
- Can exhaust themselves by giving too much to everyone else
- Takes on another person's work instead of saying "no"
- Tends to not stand up for themselves during confrontations
- Often will not share their real opinion for fear of offending you
- Can be overly empathetic, taking on others' sadness or depression

Buying Motivators

Relators are motivated by *Community*. When purchasing a product or service, they tend to consult with family, friends, or their extended social community before making a decision. They are driven to invest in their community and are more inclined to affiliate with or purchase products that give back.

Examples of Successful Relators

- Oprah Winfrey (OWN Network)
- Jimmy Fallon (The Tonight Show host)
- Bono (lead singer of U2)
- Bob Iger (former CEO, Disney Corp.)
- Mother Teresa (Caregiver)

INTELLECTUAL

Intellectuals are stimulated through books, speeches, research, reading, conversations, nature, or organization. They feel successful when accomplishing a task. They are motivated to learn, grow, and be healthy. They would rather be learning something new than just lying around. They want to better themselves and become more useful. They are driven to understand and to be more knowledgeable. They like to share what they know with others.

Strengths

- Task and goal-oriented
- Health-conscious, striving to eat healthy and be physically fit
- Intelligent and stimulated by new knowledge
- Strives to take care of the planet
- Bright, curious, and inquisitive
- Great at building systems
- Can follow step-by-step processes

Weaknesses

- Struggles with analysis paralysis
- Prone to overthinking a problem or situation
- Does not appreciate advice from others
- Feels as if they are the smartest person in the room
- Can be judgmental of others who cannot keep pace intellectually
- Can be a know-it-all
- Often gets frustrated when someone changes their schedule or is late

Buying Motivators

Intellectuals are motivated by *Systems*. When purchasing a product or service, they are looking for the details or step-by-step actions they need to take to achieve the desired goal. They want to enhance their intelligence and expertise. They desire to share what they know with others.

Examples of Successful Intellectuals

- Michelle Obama (Former U.S. 1st Lady)
- Arianna Huffington (Huffington Post)
- Jeff Bezos (Amazon)
- James Dyson (Dyson)
- Ingvar Kamprad (IKEA)

VALIDATOR

Validators feel important when they are being trusted, respected, praised, recognized, accepted, or needed. They enjoy small, intimate groups of people where they are being validated. They're often wonderful at giving validation to others. They do not like to be ignored, and they are offended when people they care about disrespect them. Validators' confidence stems from the strength of their relationships. If they feel like they are in a healthy, caring, and trusted relationship, they feel strong, secure, and loved.

Strengths

- Great at validating others
- The team motivator and cheerleader
- Strives to be trustworthy
- Respectful of others' opinions and desires
- Thrives in small, intimate social groups and settings
- Can be a team player and will support others' opinions

Weaknesses

- Does not like to be ignored
- Frustrated when people do not validate their opinion or input
- Can be needy at times
- Disappointed when people don't need them
- Can be over-trusting and be taken advantage of
- Can be jealous of others' success or accolades

Buying Motivators

Validators are motivated by giving and receiving *Admiration*. When purchasing a product or service, they are driven to use it to help others, or to help them be a better leader that people want to follow. If they buy, they want to know how it will make them look better to their peers, friends, or family.

Examples of Successful Validators

- Mark Cuban (Shark Tank)
- Ellen DeGeneres (Comedian - TV host)
- Art Linkletter (Radio and TV host)
- David Copperfield (Illusionist)

EXECUTIVE

Executives do not like to waste time. They are productive and thrive on getting the job done. They are task-oriented and focused on getting results. They do not like small talk. They are good at managing things and people. Executives feel important when they are in control, solving problems, working, providing, and winning. They are happiest when they are pursuing or achieving a desired goal.

Strengths

- Competitive and ambitious
- Have a never-say-die attitude
- Determined to win and are willing to pay the price to do so
- Like a challenge and will not flinch under pressure
- Stable, secure, and give a reassuring sense of being on solid ground
- Hard worker
- Self-starter and focused

Weaknesses

- Can be controlling by promoting their own agenda
- Frustrated when not providing at their desired level

- Cannot tolerate less productive team members and coworkers
- Can feel insecure when they are not winning
- Can be occasionally stubborn and self-centered
- Can be overly competitive and afraid of losing

Buying Motives

Executives are motivated by *Proof.* When purchasing a product or service, they want proof that it works and that it is going to make their life or business better. They respond to third-party testimonials and reviews. Executives focus on the big picture of getting what they want—not the details on how to achieve it.

Examples of Successful Executives

- Ruth Bader Ginsburg (US Supreme Court Justice)
- Michael Phelps (Olympic champion)
- Serena Williams (Tennis Player)
- Jay Z (Rapper)
- Harriet Tubman (Abolitionist and political activist)

VIRTUAL REALITY

Which sales personality do you relate with the *least*? Remember that understanding these sales motivators is a way to connect rather than divide. There is no right or wrong DRIVE, different things simply make different people tick.

The DRIVE System and virtual exams

So how exactly do you use these DRIVES and what do you focus on in order to speak their language? Let's take a look at

Directors, Relators, Intellectuals, Validators and Executives with their buying motivators, especially as relates to the orthodontic or dental practice. I'll show you solutions you can provide, areas to focus on, and sales killers for each type.

How to sell to a Director

Directors are motivated to create their ideal *Lifestyle*. When purchasing your treatment, they want to know how it is going to enhance their lifestyle or give them the life they want. They are attracted to products or services that will help them achieve financial freedom, time freedom, or give them a VIP experience. (Note: A Director is a great person to mention the "Premier Package" to. More often than not, they will pay the extra for the upgraded service.)

Directors get frustrated when they feel trapped and are not free and independent. They get bored when they are hearing the same thing over and over, so doctors and TC will want to be careful not to repeat the same thing someone else just said. Get to the point and move on. They are disappointed if they are not pursuing their life's purpose. Focus on how treatment will give them more freedom.

Director's challenges:

- They feel overwhelmed
- They do not feel free and independent
- They are not experiencing life the way they want
- They do not feel confident in their appearance

Director's solutions

When selling to a Director make sure the benefit of your product or service helps them to:

- Be free and independent
- Experience life at a whole new level (VIP experience)
- Assist them in overcoming obstacles
- Enhance their appearance

When selling to a Director

- Focus on the wow factor
- Show how it will enhance their lifestyle
- Talk about how good they will look
- Don't give them too many details
- Point out how it will make them look and feel better
- Share how it enhances their life

Things that will ruin your sale:

- Boring details
- Assigning homework
- Talking about yourself or your expertise (bragging)

Frame your treatment's benefits in a way that addresses their desire to be free and independent. Showcase how easy-to-use the program is while providing them with maximum benefit in their life, making them confident with their appearance and overcoming their challenges. If you do this, you will sell to a Director.

How to sell to a Relator

Relators are motivated by *Community*. When purchasing treatment, they tend to consult with family, friends, or their extended social community before making a decision. They are driven to invest in products that make them feel like they are part of a bigger community.

Relators are givers and often sacrifice their personal well-being for their community. They can be exhausted from taking care of everyone else. They are frustrated when they can't have an influence among their peers, friends, and family. They struggle when their relationships are not going well.

Relator's challenges:

- They feel insecure in their relationships
- They don't have the influence they want
- They feel exhausted from giving too much service
- They feel as if they are on the outside
- They are worried for their kids

Relator's solutions

When selling to a Relator make sure the benefit of your treatment helps them to:

- Have a power of influence
- Strengthen their family
- Be better parents (providing for their kids—emotionally, physically and financially)
- Deepen their relationships with their friends

When selling to a Relator

- Highlight how your product or service helps to support growing their friends/community
- Highlight how it helps connect them to others who are the same as them
- Use others' experiences and case studies
- Show how it will help more people pay attention to them

Things that will ruin your sale:

- Ignoring or not addressing the people they have brought with them
- Pressuring them to make a decision they day, as they will often consult with friends and family before making a commitment of investment
- Focusing on the "nuts and bolts"

Frame your treatment's benefits in a way that will help them be part of the "In" crowd. Focus on how it will help them connect more with friends and make it easier to create new relationships. Show how it will give them more power to influence others. If you do this, you will sell to a Relator.

How to sell to an Intellectual

Intellectuals are motivated by *Systems*. When purchasing your treatment, they are looking for the details, or step-by-step actions they need to take to achieve the desired goal. They want to enhance their intelligence and expertise. They do not want to be informed. They desire to share what they know with others.

They get frustrated when they cannot find a system to solve their problem. They have paralysis by analysis. They will exhaust themselves by creating multiple systems to solve a task. They are bothered by others who challenge or disrupt their system.

Intellectual's challenges:

- They cannot find the information they need
- They are exhausted from reading and studying too much
- Life feels too stressful to be in the moment
- They may not feel a sense of organization

Intellectual's solutions

When selling to an Intellectual, make sure the benefit of your treatment helps them to:

- Increase their knowledge
- Learn something new
- Be more organized
- Increase their health

When selling to an Intellectual

- Highlight the clear, step-by-step instructions on how to implement it in their life and get the results they want
- Tell them how they will save time and money by investing now and not waiting (especially if you have a warranty program)
- Give them a specific diagnosis and a plan, i.e. "Our bi-weekly service is the best option for you."
- Focus on how it saves them time or money and makes their life easier
- Focus on how short and direct learning curve is

Things that will ruin your sale:

- Too much focus on lifestyle and money
- Giving a weak suggestion: "Either braces or Invisalign will be ok. It's up to you."
- Discrediting them
- Looking unorganized or unsure
- Having inaccurate numbers

Frame your treatment's benefits in a way that will help them feel healthy, give clarity, stimulate them intellectually, and/or be more organized. If you do this, you will sell to an Intellectual.

How to sell to a Validator

Validators are motivated by *Admiration*. When purchasing treatment, they are driven by how it will make them look better to their peers, friends, or family. They enjoy focus and being an example people want to follow.

If you are selling to a Validator, they prefer to not be in loud, crowded places. They feel violated when people do not trust or respect them. They struggle to make a decision if there is a chance they will look stupid. They do not like to be ignored or overlooked.

Validator's challenges:

- They don't feel recognized
- They might not feel accepted
- They need to feel trusted
- They might not feel respected
- They don't feel validated
- They need to feel needed

Validator's solution

When selling to a Validator, make sure the benefit of your product or service helps them to:

- Give or receive trust
- Give or receive praise
- Give or receive respect

- Give or receive recognition
- Give or receive acceptance
- Give or receive validation

When selling to a Validator:

- Highlight how your program makes your client look and feel like a rock star
- Show them how it will bring positive attention from people
- Share how they will be able to share their experience with others seeking your service
- Highlight how it helps them look good in front of others

Things that will ruin your sale:

- If the client feels unnoticed
- If the client feels ignored
- If the client feels ignorant

Frame your treatment's benefits in a way that will help them be a giver or receiver of validation, praise, respect, acceptance, trust, recognition, and admiration. Having a friend or trusted family member in the consult, especially if they have already had a positive treatment experience, is a good thing. Use them to validate the experience. If your stories or those of a past client will validate them or their concerns, be sure to use those testimonials. If you do this, you will sell to a Validator.

How to sell to an Executive

Executives are motivated by *Proof.* When purchasing your treatment, they want proof that it works and that it is going to make their life better. They respond to third-party testimonials and reviews. Executives focus on the big picture of getting what they want—not the details on how to achieve it.

If you are selling to an Executive, they are frustrated if they are not winning and in control. They are exhausted from their enormous "To Do" list. They dislike people who waste their time and talk about nothing or repeat themselves.

Executive's challenges:

- They do not feel in control
- They are worried about making money and providing
- Exhausted from work
- They feel like there are too many problems to solve
- Feel overwhelmed from too many goals

Executive's solutions

When selling to an Executive, make sure the benefit of your treatment helps them to:

- Feel like they are winning
- Have a sense of control
- Reach their goals
- Feel a sense of security
- Solve problems

When selling to an Executive

- Does your treatment give them more control?
- Show them multiple testimonials
- Point out your accomplishments/accolades
- Give them a clear vision of how you are going to help them win
- Does it make their goals easier to achieve?
- Show what goals others have been able to achieve with your treatment

Things that will ruin your sale:

- Sharing boring details of how we do things
- Rehearsing step-by-step instructions
- Not letting them feel in control
- Not answering their questions first
- Making them feel like you don't have time for them to get the information they want

Frame your treatment's benefits to help them feel like they are winning, have a sense of control, solve problems, achieve their goals, and/or have more security. If you do this, you will sell to an Executive.

The Conversation Close

You might be thinking, "Well, this is great Dino. I love knowing what my DRIVE is but how do I figure out my clients' DRIVE so I can speak their language?"

Or at least I hope that is what you are thinking. No worries, I have you covered.

Although Woody Woodward provides more detail in his book about how to understand and successfully use your potential clients' DRIVES for their good, let's get straight to how you can use this in your presentations. It's a lot simpler than you might think. As with everything you are implementing in your business, you will need to facilitate practice and role play with your team to make it sound easy. It's called The Conversation Close.

First, you will need to discover the potential client's DRIVE so you can speak their language. In an exam room it's not ideal to ask your potential clients to do a personality assessment like we did in this chapter. Instead, here are three questions that will help you quickly identify their DRIVE.

1. Other than work and family, what are you most passionate about?

2. When you don't get to (insert Passion), how does it impact you?

3. When you get to (insert Passion), how does it make you feel?

Depending on how they answer these questions, you can get a fairly good idea of their primary DRIVE. For example, if they answer that they love to travel, be creative, experience life, overcome challenges, and feel free and independent, then they are a Director. If they talk about spending time with their family, friends, and giving back to their community or church, they are a Realtor. If their answer is organizing, exercising, eating healthy, being in nature, reading, or learning, then they are an Intellectual. If their reply is doing activities where they are being validated, respected, praised, trusted, or recognized, then they are a Validator. And lastly, if their reply has to do with winning, being in control, providing, working, achieving goals, or solving problems, then they are an Executive.

VIRTUAL REALITY

If someone were to ask you what you are passionate about, what would you say? Does your answer align with the DRIVE personality you chose?

Within one week after teaching these questions to a large DSO corporation, multiple treatment coordinators emailed me to express how much more connected they feel to their patients by using this process. One even mentioned how worried she was beforehand about sounding "weird." She expressed concern that the patients might think it's odd for her to ask these questions. However, she experienced the exact opposite. The patients were happy to answer and it made them feel like the TC really cared about them.

When you are working with kids, ask them:

1. Other than school and family, what do you love to do?
   a. 90% of the time they will say video games. Whatever their answer, follow up with:
2. What is it you love about _____ (video games or whatever they said)?

If the answer is about how good they are at video games and how they like beating the game, they are in the Executive group. If they say how much they love hanging out with their friends online and doing things together, they are in the Relator group. You get the idea.

When using the Conversation Close, if you have not been able to clarify their DRIVE, simply tie their answers to the benefit of your treatment. Connect to their passion and you will connect to their DRIVE.

Challenge #3: Take the DRIVE Quiz.

The script examples below are designed to address the potential client's primary DRIVE and should give you some good ideas on how to customize your language. At the end of each script, see if you can identify which type I am selling to and the characteristics of that type. You'll find the answers at the end.

1. "Mom, you have probably noticed that many of little Susie's classmates have been getting braces. They are much more popular today than when we were growing up. More and more parents are realizing how important it is to get straight teeth at an early age. Her smile is going to be so amazing, other kids are going to want to follow her example too."

DRIVE: _____
Characteristics: _____, _____, _____, _____

2. "We know you will see an amazing return on your investment to reach your goal of an incredible, lifelong smile. The award-winning Pitts 21™ bracket system we use is the best. They are made with the top-of-the-line materials that have been proven to get the fastest results, while not skimming on quality. Speaking of results, we have over 500 testimonials from our previous patients who are thrilled with their smiles. Dr. Awesome has also won the Best in State award for Orthodontic excellence the last 5 years running."

DRIVE: _____
Characteristics: _____, _____, _____, _____

3. "Getting treatment now is such a smart move. Not only will it save you so much in the future in the way of both time and money, it will also look amazing! Too many people put off rewarding themselves with a great smile, so good for you. A great smile is an interesting thing. People are attracted to it when they see one and they love to share it when they have one. Yours will definitely do both when we are done."

DRIVE: _____
Characteristics: _____, _____, _____, _____

4. "We have a very detailed 18-month plan that will make sure you get the best results. There are also so many long-term benefits to your health when you have a great set of teeth. If you like, we can walk you through why they are superior."

DRIVE: _____
Characteristics: _____, _____, _____, _____

5. "The amazing thing about Invisalign is the freedom you feel knowing you are getting your teeth straight, but not confined to the look of braces. Let alone the ability to eat what you want without having to worry about breaking anything. Most people will never know you have them on but you will look amazing."

DRIVE: _____
Characteristics: _____, _____, _____, _____

Answers:

1. RELATOR: Relationships, Friends, Parenting, Influence
2. EXECUTIVE: Winning, Goals, Security, Proof, 3rd Party Testimonials
3. VALIDATOR: Recognition, Praise, Validation, Respect
4. INTELLECTUAL: Knowledge, Health, Standards, Learning, Intelligence
5. DIRECTOR: Freedom, Lifestyle, Image, Appearance

Now that you know the DRIVE system, understand how to determine it through the Conversation Close, have specific tips on tips on how to sell to each type and sample scripting on how to use it in your presentation, you're ready to implement. As you practice customizing your presentation to meet your clients' needs, your connection and conversion rates will increase. Even if learning the DRIVE system simply helps you feel more confident in the sales process because you are able to identify their buying personality, that would be an incredible accomplishment.

We lose eighty percent of our sales because we are selling based on our own DRIVE and not our customer's. As you learn each patient's DRIVE, you have the potential to increase your sales by 400%.

Expert Interview:
Real World Virtual Exams with Dr. Alex Waldman

For the past two years, Dr. Alex Waldman has been making small adjustments within his Beverly Hills, California orthodontics practice. He started tackling some of his challenges with virtual solutions, taking the approach that it couldn't hurt to try something new. Technology drove innovation, which then pushed cultural change within his practice, which led to more technology, and the cycle repeated itself.

It began with technology that allowed for remote treatment of clients through dental monitoring. Waldman embraced this technology. Next his Treatment Coordinator announced that she was moving to Florida to be with her family. Waldman decided to try retaining her as a virtual TC, and she was back working full-time for him within days of her move. He now employs two others virtually, one of whom lives in the Philippines. Finally, Waldman began offering virtual orthodontic consultations to his clients, and over time has found these consults to be very effective in pre-qualifying his candidates.

He had discovered that conversion rates for internet referrals were lower than regular referrals. These people were seeking information but were often not ready to commit. So Waldman decided to work smarter, not harder. He began offering his potential clients two fantastic options: they could choose a white-glove, comprehensive in-person visit for which they would pay a fee, or they could choose a convenient virtual visit to get personalized information for free.

"Technology is important, but it's the people behind it that really matters," Waldman said. "You want to offer the patient the same feeling they would get in your office, with the same level of professionalism."

Waldman believes in tracking numbers, and he began to notice some fascinating trends as he incorporated virtual consultations. He found that about half of his potential patients were willing to pay for the in-person experience, and the other half were choosing virtual visits, saving him valuable doctor consultation time. He also found that his conversion rates for starting new adults had doubled between 2018 and 2019.

"The digital consultation is a great pre-qualifier," Waldman observed. It allowed his practice to weed out people who were not a good fit for his program. Those who made it into the office, whether through paying for an in-person consult or going through the virtual consult experience, were much more likely to commit to a treatment program.

Waldman used a product called Smile Snap to help him capture clients as they were browsing on his website. These potential clients would fill out a virtual consultation form right there on his site, even if they were in bed at 4 a.m. on a Saturday. A TC would reach out by text, phone, or even Facetime for these virtual consultations during the next business day.

"The virtual consultation, when done right, is very powerful," Waldman said. "I wasn't born with a phone in my hand so it's not intuitive for me, but for many people this is considered a more ideal option."

At first, Waldman was hesitant to share pricing over the phone. "I was taught in the year 2000, from someone trained in 1973, that you didn't share price points over the phone," he recalls. Like many professionals, he was operating on old information. He decided to take the chance and instructed his team to discuss specific options and pricing virtually. His gamble paid off. Contrary to what he had been taught, he found that when clients were given specific prices, rather than a range, his conversion rates were highest.

4

What every body is saying

"I want to encourage you all for a minute. Right now, our first responders and medical professionals are the superheroes for their bravery on the front lines. Half of my family are in this space, so they need our love and support.

"But now there's another superhero that we need to come out of this crisis.

"And that is entrepreneurs.

"Job creators. Innovators. Opportunity seekers.

"You are all going to help bring our world back from the brink of 20M unemployed. And for that, you are superheroes. You won't get any credit from anyone else, not media or politicians, maybe not even your employees or customers. In fact, you will probably get attacked or blamed for taking action now. But I know the truth. You guys are superheroes. So put on your invisible capes and keep moving."

                                                                    -Scott Donnell

During the quarantine, this quote caught my eye on social media and has been on my mind ever since. Scott Donnell runs the largest grad school fund-raising company in the country, so he knows about risk and entrepreneurship. In a time when safety concerns are paramount and fear is running rampant, the new heroes are the risk-takers who will jump-start the economy and get the world running again.

This is where you come in. Virtual business is the future, and it is approaching at a velocity unheard-of in the past. I have some radical ideas about where virtual could take us in the next 5-10 years, and I can guarantee you that you'll want to be at the forefront of this technological wave.

In this chapter, we're going to dive deep into better selling on-screen through a mastery of body language. You'll learn how to read those you communicate with, which will help you ask better questions and facilitate connection. You'll also learn to read yourself. You'll be able to look at those subtle things your body says to those around you so you can polish your message. When you know your own body, you know every body. When you focus on yourself first, you can deliver the message you want to deliver and then understand others better.

An understanding of body language will help you portray and interpret emotions clearly. Having this ability will help you in three ways. First, you'll be able to **name** the emotion that is present in your conversations. Second, you can **tame** the emotion by addressing the unspoken concerns you see in your clients. This does not mean that you call out the client's gestures, but rather that you speak to the emotion through a clarifying question or a shift in the conversation. Their subconscious will connect with that shift and help them feel calmer. Third, an understanding of body language will help you clearly **understand** how people around you are feeling. It's an incredible life tool to have in any circumstance, but especially in sales.

Everyone in your office should have a basic grasp of body language. There isn't a role that will not benefit from this knowledge. Your business will grow as your team learns to read body language in a genuine way, drawing people to want to work with you. As you build relationships, body language will help you understand how other people feel and being understood is the ultimate connection builder. People will know you care as you validate their concerns and build rapport, increasing the number of sales that you close at a higher price point.

Owners and managers

As an entrepreneur, body language is your connection to the subconscious desires of those around you. Through the insights you gain, you will be empowered to relate better with both your team and your clients. You'll be able to spot the subtle concerns early before they become big problems. You'll hire strong teams, choose amazing partners and close more clients.

One huge challenge that entrepreneurs deal with is fraud. Though the cost of fraud is difficult to calculate, it was estimated that in 2011 corporate fraud cost business owners $997 billion in the United States alone. That massive number reflects just the fraud in corporations, where there are procedures in place to monitor fraud constantly. Imagine how large that annual estimate would be if small business owners were included. It costs small business owners even more, because often the only safeguard in place to detect fraud is the owner. If that's the case in your office, the more adept you are at reading those around you, the more protected your business will be.

Salespeople

As you move towards onscreen sales, you will no longer be able to connect with clients through a high five or a handshake. Understanding body language will help you and your salespeople connect with clients even though you are not together physically.

You can learn to connect, communicate, and close over the screen. Ten years ago, having same day starts was a radical concept.

The idea was that clients needed more time to make decisions. But we are finding in our connected world that same day virtual starts are possible, and for many clients, desirable. For instance, if a prospect needs to talk to their spouse before deciding, you can reach out to the spouse on the phone during the consultation. You can create a fluid, same day close process through the screen — presenting, signing contracts and making money — and body language is going to help you make it happen.

Team members

As you share your knowledge of body language with your team, they will learn to build trust and create raving fans out of your clients. Your team is your front line in asking for referrals, so they will need to know how to connect and ask the right questions to keep your pipeline full.

Your phone ninjas can learn to listen better and understand the unspoken messages people are giving over the phone. It won't be long before the chat function on our websites becomes video-enabled and the people working the phones will be communicating onscreen. Financial team members can benefit from knowing how to hold money meetings online. Your marketing team can do Lunch and Learns virtually, sending your prospects a lunch through a delivery service and then hosting a presentation online. The shift to virtual business is going to impact every member of your team, and body language insights will be a key factor in your success.

Body Language 101

The very first televised United States Presidential Debate was held in 1960. The candidates were then Vice President Richard M. Nixon and John F. Kennedy. Because of the results of this debate, there would not be another televised presidential debate for sixteen years. Why?

In 1960, although about 80% of the population in the US had televisions, many people still used the radio to listen to their news. When the media outlets polled the country after the debate, there was a sharp divide in the results. This divide was not based along political lines like it is in our modern world, but was based on another factor.

Those who *watched* the debate overwhelmingly believed that Kennedy had won.

Those who *listened* to the debate believed that Nixon won.

There were several reasons why those who viewed the debate were in Kennedy's corner, many having to do with what people saw from both candidates. The primary cause for this rift in opinion was the negative body language cues that people observed from Nixon. (I'll show you three specific cues from that debate later on).

This disconcerting divide sparked a sixteen-year hiatus of televised debates and a new study of body language. My own journey toward mastery of this new form of communication would happen many years later.

In 2009, my wife Shannon asked me to go to a presentation she had heard of from a friend about body language. I was really not interested in going, not because I don't love hanging out with Shannon, but because the topic was not something I cared much about. I have done a lot of personal development work through books, seminars and coaching. It seemed that every time anyone talked about body language they were focused on how to tell if someone is lying to you, and that was just not interesting to me. I would rather learn how to see the positive in someone as opposed to looking for the negative. However, Shannon made me an offer I could not refuse.

She told me the location of the event was literally next door to my favorite Mexican restaurant and that if I went we could go there for dinner. The problem with being married to someone you have known since you were 5 is that they know how to push all your buttons, and she knows how much I enjoy some chips and salsa.

So of course we went.

The event was put on by a man named Kirk Duncan. One of the first reasons he gave about why learning body language was an important skill is because it helps you ask better questions of people. He didn't speak of deception or lying, but building better relationships. I loved it and Shannon and I wanted to learn more.

For the next two years we both studied and learned and even worked with Kirk to lead some of his events. We eventually went through the process of becoming certified body language experts. (In full disclosure Shannon got hers first, but there was no way I was going to be married to someone who understood body language that well and not learn it myself. I am not a foolish man, after all.)

Understanding body language has helped us in so many ways and has been something I feel lucky to share with my clients and their teams.

Body language, like any other language, is a learned skill. You could say that it is the very first learned skill of all of humanity — the hidden message in a parent's touch, the posture of a sibling, the look on someone's face. Most people consider themselves to be good at body language. In a recent survey, I asked people how well they thought they read body language. Over 60% responded that they were naturally gifted at understanding body language without any sort of formal training.

Well, I'm here to tell you that you aren't naturally gifted at understanding body language. It's the very subtle things in body language that count, and like any other learned skill, you need to study and hone it before it can be a useful tool for you. Believing that you can understand this language organically is almost like believing that you can spot the difference between Chinese and Japanese dialects without study. Well, you can try. But your results will be much better with a little guidance.

We'll start with a quick test. Imagine you are hosting a holiday party for your office, and in a grand show of gallantry you've invited me to attend. As the festivities progress, you notice me standing with my arms folded. What is my body language telling you?

When I ask this question, I get all kinds of different answers. Most commonly people believe that I am bored, ready to leave, or feeling guarded. But the truth is, without context, you have no idea what I am thinking or feeling. Maybe I'm just cold!

From my experience, the number one rule of body language is that there is no right or wrong interpretation, just weak or strong interpretation. When we are attempting to better understand others through their body language, we need to take out judgment. Instead, we are looking for clusters of behaviors to give us clues and help us to ask insightful questions.

Oftentimes people will observe specific movements and ask, "What does 'X' mean?" The challenge is that it's not that simple. Body language is not an exact science. If it were, experts would be able to tell if a person was telling the truth or lying with precision. Rather, body language is an important tool to help us ask better questions and it's not 100% accurate every time.

A study by Mehrabian & Ferris Research in 1967 revealed that when humans communicate with each other, they express just 7% of their meaning through the spoken word, 38% through tone of voice, and a full 55% through body language. Interestingly enough these stats, although often quoted as I just did, are not entirely accurate. Over the years there have been various concerns about the accuracy of those numbers when they are presented as a blanket statement of fact. Mehrabian himself wrote in his 1972 book *Nonverbal Communication* that these numbers were generated from a specific situation and did not represent a universal truth. However, he also wrote, "When there are inconsistencies between attitudes communicated verbally and posturally, the postural component should dominate in determining the total attitude that is inferred."

In other words, those numbers work when there is an incongruence between the message and the physicality. As an obvious example, if you ask someone how they are doing and their words and their disposition match through a wide smile, then both their words and their body are in alignment. However, if someone just fell and scraped their knee and they answer, "I am fine," while hopping around in agony, then there is a mismatch and the message is incongruent.

Another differentiator would be if someone is engaging in an emotional topic vs. a technical one. If it's a technical topic, the majority of their message is most likely not coming from their non-verbal cues. That is not to say there are no non-verbal cues, but the majority of the communication will be verbal.

Even with these clarifications, the study is important because we often put a lot of stock in the words that are coming out of our mouths and not near enough emphasis on understanding what our bodies are saying. Just consider the meaning communicated through tone of voice. Your tone is a fantastic conveyor of emotion. Just imagine the possible meanings of the sentence, "Honey, take out the trash." The meaning could be anything from a loving reminder to a weighty threat, and all conveyed through tone.

The bulk of the messages we are communicating to others is happening through the movement of our bodies. The body is a billboard that is constantly sending out messages. Studies have shown that people are capable of thinking at an average speed of 450 words per minute. This average speed can be slower for some men and faster for some women, but we are all incapable of speaking at these types of speeds. The words we cannot speak are going to manifest themselves through our body language.

Your subconscious mind churns out all of these thoughts and the conscious mind filters what we will vocalize to about 150 words per minute. However, thoughts have weight, and those 300 unspoken words that were filtered out can be subconsciously expressed through body language.

These messages will be portrayed using different parts of our bodies, because our thoughts are connected to certain areas of the body. As an example, my sister-in-law recently suffered from a mini stroke. It was a mild episode of numbness on her left side and some heart concerns. If you think back to biology class, you might remember that the right hemisphere of the brain is associated with the left side of the body, so her stroke occurred on the right side of her brain. Because of that association between the areas of the brain and the areas of the body, we can learn to decode body language.

If I were to ask you which part of the body you notice first when you meet someone, you would probably answer, "Their eyes." Most people believe that they look at another person's eyes first, but science tells a different story. So if your brain is not noticing the eyes first, what does it notice?

The image below, strange as it may appear, is an illustration of the order of importance the brain sees when looking at another human being.

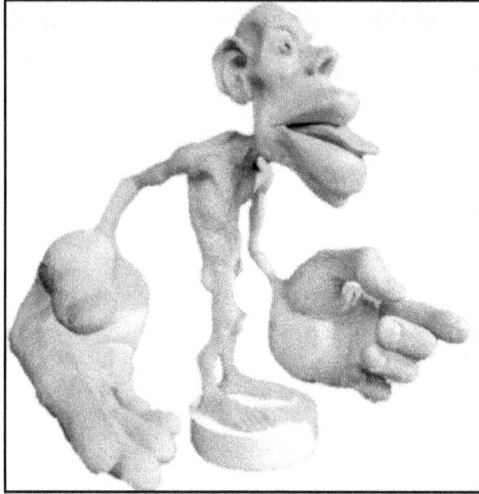

Dr. Wilder Penfield was a brain surgeon in the 1930's. He studied people with epilepsy and performed surgeries on their brains to try and find a cure. During his surgeries he took the opportunity to perform tests on various parts of the brain. In doing so, he was able to find out which sections of their cerebral cortex controlled which bodily functions and feelings. From those experiments, he discovered a very distorted view of the human body based on how the brain focuses. He called it the "cortical homunculus".

Notice how the hands, lips, tongue and feet are disproportionately large compared to the other body parts? We will be focusing on specific body parts and how to understand them better. Let's delve into a few of the most telling body parts and how they can help us connect through the screen.

VIRTUAL REALITY

Don't let a better understanding of body language make you self-conscious. As an adult, your patterns of behavior have been developing over decades. Give yourself and those around you some grace.

SHOULDERS

The message conveyed by shrugging shoulders is the number one overlooked and underused body language tell. If you watch people closely, you'll see the shoulders frequently convey mixed messages in conversations. A person will say one thing, but their shoulders will tell a different story.

Shrugging the shoulders gives a message of uncertainty. Sometimes the words a person uses matches the uncertainty of a shoulder shrug. For example, if I ask you what you want for dinner and you shrug and say, "I don't know," your verbal and nonverbal language are consistent. However, If I ask you how much you love your new boyfriend and you shrug and say, "I totally love him. We're going to be together forever," I can deduce that there is more to the story than you are telling. The language you are using and the language I am seeing in your body are incongruent. I know that's a bit of an exaggerated example, but if you watch you will see that people often indicate mixed messages through shrugging.

Go to https://dinowatt.com/mve-bonus/ to watch the full example video.

Usually shrugging is very subtle. Sometimes only one shoulder will move up and down. When I first began speaking onstage, I would watch recordings of myself afterwards and noticed that I tended to shrug my right shoulder when I was not quite sure if I were sharing the right statistic or answering a question correctly. Shrugs don't make sense when they occur during a statement of surety.

One sales example of shoulder shrugging involves Hannah, our college student who is considering braces. During the sales presentation I explain to Hannah that she will have to wear the Invisalign product for 22 hours each day. When I ask her how she feels about that, she says it sounds okay while shrugging. As soon as I notice the shrug, I immediately ask her if there is anything she is uncertain about. She then shares with me that she often travels for work and is unsure how she will take the retainers out to eat and brush her teeth. Noticing that shrug gives us the chance to talk about the concern until she sorts it out in her mind, and then we move on.

A more rare occurrence is a massive shoulder shrug, which is actually a primal defense move to protect the neck. When you see this type of behavior in a client or team member, it is indicative that something more significant is going on. Perhaps the person does not believe you or feels defensive for some reason.

When you notice the inconsistency in what your clients say and what they do, allow them to voice their concern. It sets them at ease, allowing them to mentally move past the issue. Often a client will say what you want them to say because they want to be nice and don't want to disappoint you. They might not quite understand what is being asked. Shoulder shrugging does not indicate outright dishonesty, but rather a conflict of feelings that you can help sort out, freeing them to move forward.

HANDS

What to do with your hands

Hands are one of the most expressive parts of our bodies because they are our secondary communication devices. Hands are strong indicators of energy level and attentiveness. As you practice your onscreen presence, it is essential to keep your hands as visible as possible. You'll want to adjust your camera distance and angle to allow plenty of room to record your hand gestures.

The reason for this is that when weighing our relationships with others, the subconscious mind looks at the hands first. The caveman brain looks for the hands because the hands tell a story: is this person going to feed me, or kill me? That primal brain will see a person with his hands in his pockets and wonder what he is hiding. There is a subconscious drop in trust when you cannot see someone's hands. To gain your clients' trust, you'll want your hands to be visible and to use them intentionally.

I use my hands every time I talk about money. When I am referring to a price range I space my hands apart, and then when I am talking about the actual purchase price I bring them closer together.

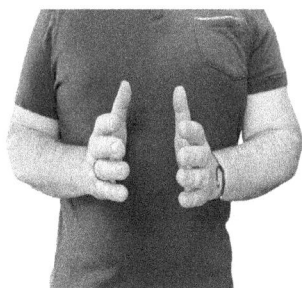

"I know you are offering $500."   "All I can offer is $300."

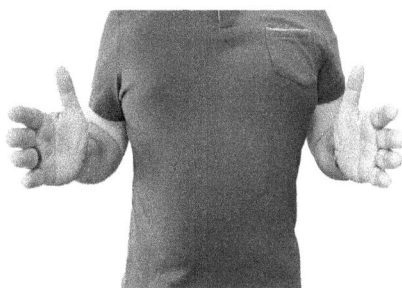

This may seem like an insignificant thing, but the brain picks up on those cues. You can practice expressing through your hands with your kids until you get the hang of it. When you are talking about an opportunity you space your hands wide to indicate how great it is, and when you are talking about the small sacrifice they will have to make to earn it you'll bring your hands closer together. See if it's easier to get them to clean their rooms before you have an amazing time at the water park through using your hands.

What their hands can tell you

When I am having a conversation with a client or team member, I always watch for soothing hand gestures as an emotional indicator. Sometimes a person will hold their hands together and massage them. They might use one hand to rub the opposite shoulder, arm or leg. Women will often indicate discomfort by rubbing the suprasternal notch, or the central dip where the neck meets the torso. Pacifying behaviors also include rubbing watches or earrings, playing with necklaces, cracking knuckles, or biting lips or fingers.

Covering up or rubbing your Suprasternal Notch is a clear soothing cue. Watch how she combines with another hair play

Go to https://dinowatt.com/mve-bonus/ to watch the full example video.

Pacifying behavior originates from our time as babies. Babies are often comforted through rubbing, patting and massage. When we exhibit soothing behaviors, we are simply attempting to replicate that same sense of calm that we experienced in our infancy when a parent was rubbing our back.

| Rubbing of arm | Rubbing top of hand | Rubbing leg or knees | Rubbing back of neck |

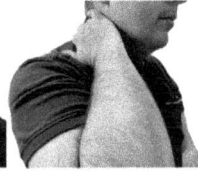

Consider what you do with your body while in the dentist chair. Whenever I am in this uncertain space, I will clasp my hands, hold them to my chest, and rub my fingers. This is my body's way of attempting to hold my emotions in.

When you see pacifying behaviors in your prospective clients, it's time to slow down, allow a brief pause in the conversation, and then ask what is concerning the client. If you are a talker like me, you may have to force yourself to pause, but it is so important to the relationship if you do so. Pausing and seeking to understand the client is a great rapport-builder as you will be addressing the client's unspoken concern. Their mind will automatically pick up on how well you understand them, and they will often open up to you about what is bothering them. You can offer an explanation or repeat what you said previously to come to an understanding, then move on together when it feels like their concern has been resolved.

My wife, Shannon, had an impactful experience with hands and self-soothing at the dentist office. For some reason Shannon's body needs a heavy dose of medication to combat pain, and the medication tends to cycle through her system so quickly that she often needs an additional dose. She knows this about herself and tries to communicate it to medical professionals. At a recent dental appointment to replace an old filling, the dentist attempted to give Shannon a higher dosage. However, when he inserted the appliance to hold her mouth open, she could still feel the metal against her mouth. The dentist began working on her tooth and she knew he would be working deep, close to the nerve. She began to feel extreme anxiety. Though she has a great mindset and knows many mindfulness techniques to combat these fears, she was also using her hands to self-soothe. Though her pacifying movements should have been obvious to the dental staff, they were not paying attention to her body language and had no idea what she was communicating.

Shannon is an adult, and she knows how to advocate for herself. She was able to communicate with the staff and they gave her a headset with classical music to help ease her mind throughout the procedure. But many other people, including children, are less able to verbally communicate these types of anxieties. As a professional, you want to become fluent in understanding these non-verbal cues.

Whenever you see a client or a patient self-soothe, whether it's tapping their feet or rubbing their hands, don't just ask if everything is okay. You need more than just a yes or no question to help them feel more at ease. You already know they are not okay because you can see what is happening through their body language. A better question is to ask how you can help the person feel better. Something like, "I can see that you are nervous, what can I do to help you feel better?" Different things will help different people feel more comfortable, so the more options you have, the better.

Relationship building is key. At the end of the day, it won't matter to your clients how beautiful your office is or how technologically advanced your tools are or how many degrees you hold, if you are unable to meet their emotional needs. Relationship building is that important, and hands are a huge tell when it comes to how others are feeling. Pay attention to the hands to help your clients have the best experience possible.

EYES

What to do with your eyes

Watching peoples' eyes is my favorite part of reading body language. You can tell so much about where a person is coming from by watching their eyes during a conversation. Whether you are aware of it or not, your eyes show where you are getting your information from. As you speak, you will literally glance at the part of the brain you are accessing. It's an incredible asset in your relationships to be able to read where people are getting their information from. I'll teach you how to decode your clients' eye movements in the next section.

When the goal is to connect, eye contact is crucial. And selling through the screen actually makes observing eye movements easier than selling in person. When you are conversing through the screen you have a concentrated time and space so it's easier to pay attention. You literally put your client into a small frame that you can focus on. Eye contact is an important channel that you will want to keep open. Eyes convey information about attention and interest that you can use to regulate the flow of the conversation. People who make eye contact convey interest, concern, wealth and credibility. You'll want to learn how to maintain that channel of communication through your eyes.

If you have a client who is breaking eye contact, you don't have to be weird about it and try to force them to maintain your gaze. If the eyes of the person on your screen are darting all over and they don't want to look at you for some reason, just try to let them lead and follow their rhythm. You can practice making eye contact more natural, and when someone looks away occasionally you can break away, too. It's almost like taking a breath. For those of us who have a little ADD and our brains are all over the place, sometimes it can be exhausting to focus on one thing for a long time. Just match the client but remain open and gentle with your eyes.

Whenever you are listening to a client, practice actively raising your eyebrows to indicate that you are paying full attention to them. This eye flare conveys interest and clues them in to engage with you in the conversation.

When a client has a concern, you might furrow your brow and tilt your head a little. This movement will indicate a lack of understanding and encourage the client to explain the concern fully. When this exchange happens, the client often becomes more focused on helping you understand than the concern itself.

They may be ready to move on in the conversation once they have felt heard.

What their eyes can tell you

Your clients' eyes will show you what is influencing their answers and decisions. As you learn to read and understand eye movements, you will be empowered to ask the right questions and have smoother conversations and closes.

Everyone uses every part of the brain, and neuroscience has shown us that different information is stored in different areas of the brain. We are going to focus on five major eye movements to help you better understand whether your clients are driven by the right brain, the left brain, an outside influence, higher thoughts or lower thoughts.

When a client's eyes look up and to their right, they are accessing thoughts from their **right brain**. This is the futuristic side of the brain and is the center for creativity. When a client is looking at the right brain, they are seeing a vision of what may be. For instance, if you are selling real estate and you ask the client if they can picture themselves in a house, they may look to their right brain to access that futuristic information. If you ask your kid if they cleaned their room and they look at their right brain, you can bet they are being a little creative with their answer, so you may want to ask more specific follow-up questions. The right brain knows what to do, it can see that vision or goal.

The **left brain** is going to show you how to do it. The left brain is the part of the brain that stores past information and is the center for logic. When someone looks up and to the left, they are looking into their past at what happened before for evidence. When you ask a client what sort of monthly payment they can afford and they glance up and to the left, you'll know they have calculated from their experience to get to this answer. If they look to the right, you'll know they are envisioning the answer and you may need to ask a follow-up question to get more clarity.

When a person glances straight at their ear on either side, they are listening to an **outside influence**. We all have outside influences that drive our decisions, from a spouse or parent to the news. If someone is glancing at their ear, an outside influence is the most important voice to them. If you ask a client if they are ready to buy a house and they glance at their ear, it is highly likely they want to consult with someone else before they can fully make that decision. When you see this behavior in a client, go ahead and ask if there is someone else that it would be good to check with before making a final decision.

When a person looks **straight up**, they are tapping into their higher brain function or their higher spiritual power. This is where people look for inspiration and hope, and it's where most of us do our best thinking. The next time you have a problem, try looking up so you can access more of these higher thoughts.

When a person looks **down**, they are looking into their soul at their feelings. If you see someone looking down, try to address feelings rather than thoughts. A lot of emotion is stored in the top part of the body near the heart and sometimes people need to look at this space to make a decision.

An example of looking down comes from my experience as a dad. I remember asking my son if he would like a peanut butter cookie or a chocolate chip cookie and he looked down. I had learned from my own childhood that this was a sign of disrespect, so I instructed my son to look me in the eye when he was talking to me. It wasn't until later that I realized he wasn't disrespecting me; he was simply looking at his emotion and his soul to find his answers. A lot of the time kids make their decisions through their feelings, so I learned to adjust my approach. When I allowed him to look down, he could find the answer and was less likely to regret it. You can see that the ability to understand non-verbal communication is going to strengthen your relationships, and not just in the office.

When we make our best decisions, it is through checking in with our higher thoughts to make sure they match our emotions. If a client is stuck and unable to decide, ask them to look up for the answer. Ask them to look down or maybe close their eyes for a moment. These simple motions can unlock thoughts and feelings that will lead to solid decision-making.

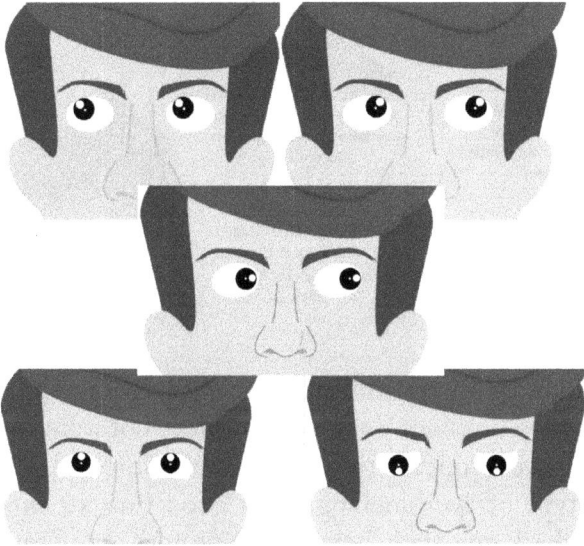

Another eye tell in sales is eye blocking. Sometimes a person will cover the eyes or close them for an extended period of time. Be on the lookout for eye closing, long blinks, avoiding eye contact, shielding eyes with objects and forehead touching.

Eye Blocking

Closing eyes can indicate:

1. Trying to shut the visual out so they can concentrate on the question/ statement.
2. Not wanting to see what is in front of them, or not wanting to be seen.

Pinching of bridge of nose covering eyes with eyebrows furrowed:

1. Form of intense focus on the topic and showing they are interested.
2. Trying to block the data. Too intense for them to look at.

Using Hand to Forehead: Sense of shame. Possibly about money or lack in their life.

Eye blocking usually indicates one of two things: it can mean that the person does not want to see or does not want to be seen. They may have a concern that needs to be addressed. When you spot this type of eye blocking, it's a good time to slow down, explain and ask questions before moving forward. Eye blocking can also simply mean they need to take a moment to block out the world and think. If this is the case, their eyes might look upward. When you see this behavior in a client, be sure to pause and allow them that moment to think. It's an important part of their process, so learn how to pause when they are thinking!

It's a good idea to roleplay different scenarios involving eye blocking to better understand if the person needs more information to address their concern or simply a pause in the conversation. As you practice you will want to pay attention to the eye blocking, recognize the message, and adjust your response accordingly.

Money is a great emotion driver. Whenever the conversation turns to money, look for changes in body language such as subtle eye blocking movements like touching the forehead. When you notice this nonverbal message, address the concerns right away. Don't keep presenting and allow the client to remain in those emotions of shame or embarrassment. Instead, talk about the flexibility of your payment options. As you make sure the client feels comfortable and understood, it will help to dissipate any fear of not being able to make the payment.

What to say to alleviate payment concerns: "The good news is we have many options around payment to make it easy for you."

What not to say: "Hey, I noticed you put your hand to your forehead. You must be ashamed or embarrassed."

The idea here is to speak *to* the body language, not *about* the body language. When you do this, you are telling their subconscious that you see the message they are trying to convey, and you understand it. Internally, they will be impressed by your ability to name and tame their emotion without their having to say anything.

I recently gave a body language presentation in a mastermind called the Genius Network. Another member of the group is Chris Voss. If you don't know who Chris is, you should. He is a former FBI hostage negotiator and author of the must-read book, *Never Split the Difference*. After my presentation, Chris shared a general question that he uses when he notices body language shifts in another person. And anytime Chris is going to give me a suggestion on how to connect with people and be more effective, I am going to listen. Better yet, I am going to pass it along to you.

When you see a movement happen, simply make the statement, "*It seems like something has just crossed your mind.*" Then pause and let them answer.

Making this statement will prompt the person to answer without pointing out anything specific and potentially make them defensive. The great thing about this question is that it can apply to any area of body language movement, not just the eyes. For example, the lips. Which is our next area of focus.

LIPS

The next non-verbal cue to watch for is the lips. The lips can tell you if someone has a question, if they don't like what you are saying or if they don't understand you.

People will press their lips together to indicate that they want to say something. If you see a client press their lips together so entirely that the lips disappear completely, you've talked for too long without allowing for a response.

The problem with that is if they have something to say and you do not recognize it or address it, they will stop listening to you because their mind is focused on the questions they have which are not being answered.

Here is a typical evolution of the lips you can see when someone has a question or something to say.

When they have something to say or a question to ask:

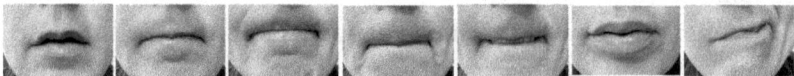

1.	2.	3.	4.	5.	6.	7.
Natural Lip Placement can have a slight opening or the lips can lightly touch.	Watch for an inhale as they move from a natural placement to a closed mouth.	Waiting for the right moment to speak.	Tightening the lips to hold in what they want to express.	Literally "biting their lips" trying not to innterrupt.	In an effort for relief, they may sigh or "exhaust" out the thought.	They don't believe you or they are annoyed with you.

When it comes to people not liking what they hear, the more their lips will collapse inward. Here is a good rule of thumb. "When you don't like what you see or hear, your lips disappear."

It doesn't necessarily mean they don't like you; they simply have a concern and the subconscious is giving you an indicator of that concern. So, make sure you address it.

Go to https://dinowatt.com/mve-bonus/ to watch the full example video.

This is something we all do. The moment we have something to say, but it's not the right time or place, our lips will tighten up in preparation for the opportunity to express ourselves.

Kids are fantastic examples of this behavior. When you are speaking to a kid and they want to talk, they will play with their lips or cover them with their hands, physically preventing themselves from speaking. We do the same thing as adults when we want to say something, but we try to be a little more tactful about it.

If you are carefully observing a client's lips, you can often tell the exact moment in the conversation where a concern crops up. Again, instead of pushing forward to the next segment of your presentation, stop and create a space for your clients to express themselves.

No need to make a big deal out of it, but as soon as you can, finish the point you were making and ask, "So, what questions or thoughts do you have about that?" When it comes to getting people to trust you, recognizing that they have something to say, even if their subconscious is doing the talking, is a great way to do so.

FACE

There are a few other body language tells that can help us navigate our conversations better by reading our clients' faces. If you are ever talking with someone and you notice them scratching their **ears**, this behavior often means that they are not able to hear you. You might check in and make sure they can hear your voice. You might speak up a little, move closer to the microphone or adjust your mic volume.

When you see a person touching their **nose** during a conversation, this may indicate that they might not believe you. The nose is one of the most sensitive places on the body and scratching the nose could mean they are having a hard time wrapping their mind around that statistic or idea. If you see nose rubbing, you might reiterate the information in a different way. You can even use, "Though this might be hard to believe," to signal to their subconscious that you understand their skepticism and help them believe.

If you see a person rub their **eyes**, this is an indication that they might not be able to see or understand what you are saying. Maybe you just talked about a heavy piece of data that they don't understand. You will need to spend a little more time explaining yourself to make sure they understand your point.

The **breath** is another clue that you'll need to be aware of. As you are speaking in front of any audience, live or onscreen, breath is an indicator of your level of interest in them. When you are short of breath, it indicates that you are thinking of yourself and getting your message out more than you are thinking of your audience understanding your message. Quick, breathless segments indicate self-absorption. Before you begin speaking, take a couple of deep breaths. Think about your audience, whether it's your clients or your team. It's all about them. This will convey a sense of trust as you speak and then pause to allow them to think about your message. The inverse of this tactic is employed by the used-car salesman who has to speak so fast and breathlessly that prospective buyers have no time to think for themselves. When you speak, remember there is a pause at the end of each of your sentences and breathe deliberately.

Speaking of breathing, watch for exhausts of breath. When someone forces out a large amount of air from their lungs, especially after some questioning, there is usually a bit of emotion that goes along with it. Sometimes it can indicate relief that they just got away with something. They may have been holding something back and when you didn't ask about it, their brain is relieved and they audibly exhaust the breath.

When someone forces out or let's out a large amount of air from their lungs, especially after some questioning, there is usually a bit of emotion that goes along with it. Sometimes it can indicate that they just got away with something or were holding something back but you didn't ask about it so they, "exhausted" it once their brain thought it was over.

As you present to your clients, be watching what they do before, during, and after the body movement tells. You'll never go wrong when reading body language if it helps you to ask better questions.

I have a good friend in the financial world who I admire for his great character. I once attended a convention where he was a speaker and I observed something. He was up on stage talking about his experience with banks being deliberately underhanded and untrustworthy. While he was speaking about these banks, I watched him scratch his nose. Now, I knew that he was a person of integrity, but I also knew that people in the audience might subconsciously pick up on that cue and doubt his trustworthiness. I was sure to have a conversation with him afterwards and warn him about it. A few times I've been training in front of an audience and my nose started itching so badly that I asked the audience to turn to their neighbors and interact briefly, just so I could scratch my nose.

These cues are simple and quick. They might even seem a little silly until you remember that the bulk of our thoughts are communicated through body language. Don't ignore these indicators. As you connect with others, pay attention to their hands, eyes, shoulders, lips and face. Practice observing body movement to better understand and meet the needs of those around you.

GETTING PAST THE MASK

We've all heard the saying from Shakespeare's Sonnets that the eyes are the windows to the soul. Since COVID-19 descended, the eyes can be the driving force behind powerful communication and relationship building now more than ever. Let's examine how you can use your eyes to speak more clearly and how to better understand others through theirs.

One of the positive aspects of wearing a mask is that it forces you to focus on the eyes and to communicate with others more effectively through your eyes. As more and more of us are required to wear masks both in and outside of the office, it's important that you learn how to convey your message to the person that you're talking to.

A few years ago, there was a procedural show on television called *Lie to Me*. It was based upon the work of Dr. Paul Ekman who is a world-renowned researcher and the father of understanding micro expressions in the face. Micro expressions are the split-second emotional movements that happen in the face and are expressed universally by everyone. This poses a challenge; unless you are actually looking for them, micro expressions are not consciously noticeable. However, if you train yourself to look for them, you will increase your ability to have more meaningful and connective conversations.

There are seven basic expressions: happiness, surprise, disgust, sadness, contempt, fear, and anger. How can we possibly see all of these expressions when half of the face is covered up with the mask? Well, there are a few tell-tale signs that you can look for in the eyes that will help you uncover what they are actually saying. I'm also going to share with you some of the vocal tones that you might hear with each of these expressions. To break things down a bit for you, it's easier if you focus on what I call the trifecta of the face: the brows, the eyelids and the muscles around the eyes. Look for these three cues to know what expressions they are having.

Fear. When a person is expressing fear, the eyebrows tend to flatten and the forehead elongates a little bit. The eyelids widen up to see what's going on. The voice of a fearful person is going to get deeper and sharper and faster in its speech.

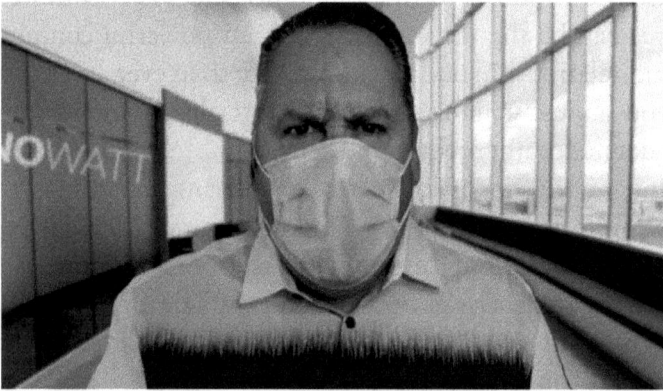

Surprise. When someone experiences surprise, the eyebrows arch and the forehead lines become crinkled. The mask might elongate as the cheeks flatten down because everything is getting longer in the face. Surprise can be a negative or a positive thing depending on the situation. For example, surprise might be a negative thing if it occurs during a contract negotiation or while reading through an agreement. The person might have an eye flare while they are reading something and their eyes will quickly widen in surprise. The vocal tone in surprise is usually going to be a higher pitch that stays high and may get louder as they are talking.

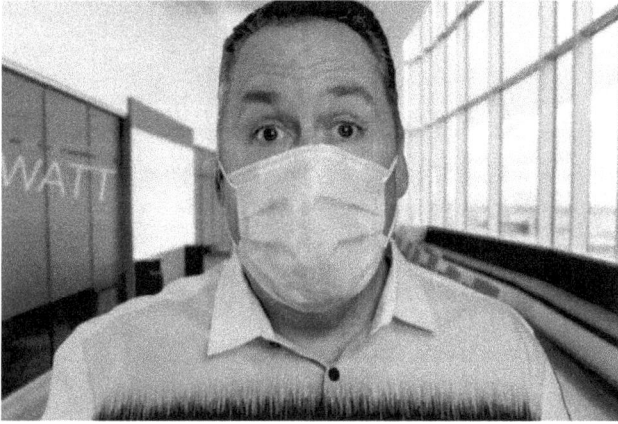

Anger. Anger will cause the lines between a person's brow and their lower lids to harden. The sides of the mask are probably going to suck in a little bit because they are bringing everything in. An angry tone is going to be forced, loud and staccato.

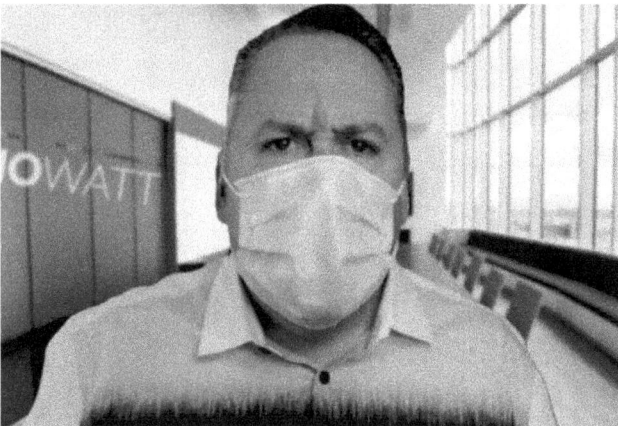

Happiness. You can see if someone is genuinely happy and joyful as you watch their eyes. You'll notice a difference between someone who is feigning happiness or really is happy by the wrinkles on the sides of the eyes. The eyes get smaller, the upper cheek muscles will elevate, and you will see the wrinkles by the eyes of a happy person. The tone is very light and the sound will go up at the end of the sentence.

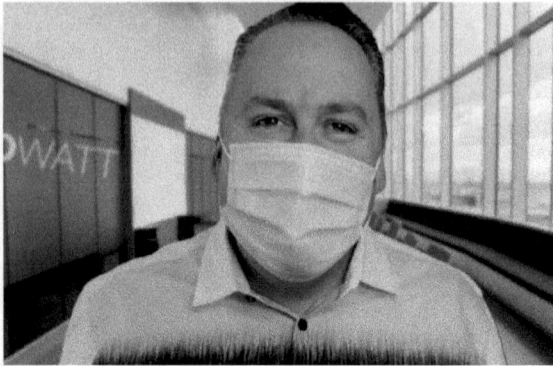

Disgust. Disgust looks a little bit like anger, but you'll notice that the upper nose will crinkle more than the brows will. The brows will get a bit sharper, but the nose is where you are going to see disgust the most. The disgust response comes from the same type of movement for when you smell something bad, and that cue will occur in the upper nose. The tone is very nasal with elongated phrases.

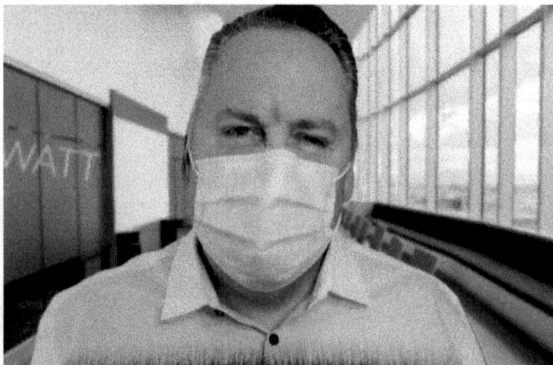

Contempt. While contempt is difficult to see if you can't see the whole face, there's a tell-tale sign for contempt: when someone rolls their eyes. An eye-roll is a sign of a person feeling like they are less-than and need to make the other person feel weaker. Think about how you feel when people roll their eyes at you. It's unsettling and can bring on self-doubt, making you feel less-than, which is exactly what a contemptuous person is going for. The tone rolls with the words, as in, "Oh, yeah, sure." They may also make an exhaust sound or you might hear total sarcasm.

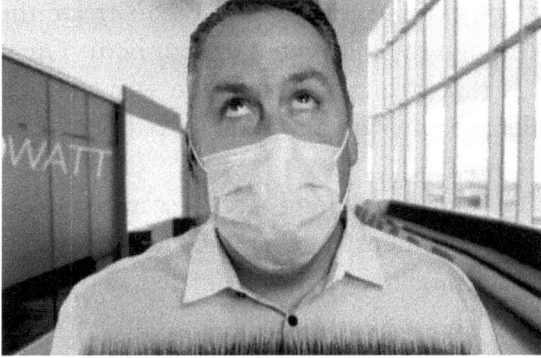

Sadness. When expressing sadness, the eyebrows flatten out and pinch where they meet the nose. The eyelids are going to droop down and often they look mis-matched. A sad tone takes on a lower inflection, is breathier, and has a slower pace.

Remember, as with anything else, you need to practice watching for these cues so that you can get better at recognizing them. Then follow up with better questions that help the person talking with you feel more connected with you. As you watch those around you for these expressions, you will have better communication with everyone in your life.

For a six minute video on how to read the eyes when people are wearing masks, go to https://dinowatt.com/mve-bonus/.

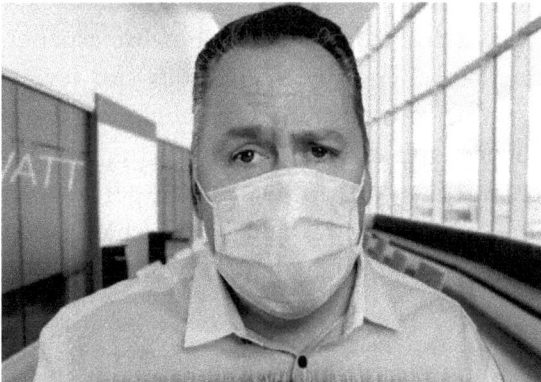

Reverse engineering with body language

Once you begin to understand how the thoughts we don't speak show up in body language, it is possible to create the thoughts you desire through the movement of your body. The mind-body connection is that strong. Through the way you hold yourself, you can influence emotion and thought patterns, and I'm going to show you how.

In 2010, Harvard University researcher, Amy Cuddy, conducted an experiment to gain more knowledge of how movement affects hormone levels. They created a scenario where the subjects played a gambling game involving risk while being monitored for changes in hormone levels. However, half of the subjects were instructed to hold a power pose (like a superhero pose) for five minutes before the game began. The other half of the subjects were instructed to hold their bodies in a disempowered pose (like slumping the shoulders). The difference in hormones levels for these two groups was astonishing.

The test group that held power poses were 86% more likely than the other group to take risks during the course of the game. The power pose group's hormone levels indicated a 25% decrease in cortisol (which is the stress hormone), and a 19% increase in testosterone (the confidence hormone). The group that held disempowered poses? Their cortisol (stress) levels increased by 17% and testosterone (confidence) went down by 10%. If you can imagine the emotion that those hormone levels represent, you will begin to understand that the way we hold ourselves as we move through life has a dramatic impact on how we experience life.

Practicing body language techniques can reverse engineer what is happening in your brain. It can help you feel better, have more confidence, and deal with stress better. You'll have more clarity when working with others. You'll get tripped up less if you fall behind. Your body language will change your behavior and the perception that others have of you.

The Power of the Power Pose

Think back on the times that you have experienced energy and presence before. Have you ever been in a room and felt like the energy got sucked out of the space because of just one person's presence? Have you felt the positive energy go out like a vacuum? You've also likely felt the reverse; the vibrant energy that comes into a room when just one person enters it. As human beings we're all going to experience the entire gamut of emotion, and it takes some practice to be that high-energy person in the room that people are going to be attracted to.

Start today to use body language to change your emotions. You can reverse engineer your thoughts using what I call a power interrupt. The key is to move into a power pose! Take a moment right now and throw your shoulders back. Breathe deeply and situate yourself into a powerful pose. Don't rush it and don't be embarrassed about it! The confidence will flow from the cues of your body.

This is a technique you will want to practice every time you are in front of the screen. Stand in front of the camera and take a moment to get your body ready. Keep your shoulders back and hold your chest up to draw that confidence to you. Amazing as it may seem, the way we experience life is an accumulation of hundreds of small habits that we make every day. These micro-habits shape our actions and behaviors in profound ways and adjusting just a few of them can have a tremendous impact. It might be helpful for you to put a note by your camera or find another trigger to remind you about power pose. Taking those 30 seconds to intentionally position yourself before going live will have profound results.

VIRTUAL REALITY

What will your go-to power pose be?
Who does this specific pose make you feel like?

Are you still wondering what happened in the Nixon vs. Kennedy debate that had people coming to such extreme conclusions depending on whether they viewed or listened to the candidates?

Here are three cues that Nixon communicated with his body before the arguments had even started. From the very beginning of the debate, his body language did him no favors.

His eyes: We tend to look at the person with the most authority in the room. Here Nixon is looking at Kennedy as if to be giving him that title.

His hand: It looks like he is holding on for dear life to that chair with his left and clenching his leg with the right. He doesn't look relaxed at all. Also, it looks like he is making a fist which is not welcoming or open. Remember, our hands are our secondary communication device.

His feet: Does he look like he wants to stick around for the debate or does he look like he wants to run out of there? When a person wants to leave, their feet are often the first thing their brain communicates with. When all the brains watching this debate saw Nixon's feet, they probably noticed that he was ready to get out of this situation as soon as he could.

Remember the results of this debate were so profound that not another was held for sixteen years. You can watch the entire debate on YouTube and see why the results were so dramatic with your new eye for body language.

One of the greatest gifts we have in our technological age is the ability to watch ourselves on video. Now it's your turn to see what your body is saying with your next challenge.

Challenge 4A: Evaluate your story video.

It's time for a second challenge! You are going to need all of your confidence for this one, so first take a second to take a picture of yourself while you are doing your power pose. You can pose like you just put on your superhero cape, flex those muscles or do a yoga warrior pose. Snapping that picture will help you get over the seeming silliness of it and into a position for that positive energy to flow!

Now that you are in a confident place and feeling good, it's time to pull up the video footage of the story that you posted on social media during the first challenge. That's right, you're going to use your new-found knowledge of body language to watch yourself tell your story. Your shoulders, hands, eyes, lips and face will reveal the rest of the story that your body is telling those around you.

Watching recordings of yourself speaking or selling is almost like a football team watching game footage to perfect their game. The purpose is not to critique, but to gather information and see what you can improve on in the future. How is your camera angle? Are you able to see your hands? How was your eye contact? Did your shoulders or your lips tell a different story than your words did? How do you hold yourself?

As you are watching yourself, please beware of perfectionism. For those of you who consider yourself perfectionists or have perfectionistic tendencies, let me offer you this perspective. I have observed that perfectionists are really imperfectionists. The truth is that they live in an imperfectionist state. Perfectionists don't walk around enjoying the life around them — instead, they are constantly looking for a way that things could be better. They don't take in the beauty of a vase of flowers, but instead rearrange them. If this is the mindset that you tend towards, I invite you to let it go. I invite you to look at imperfection as the new perfect, because perfection is a myth. Give yourself the gift of allowing imperfection to be enough so you can get started.

Remember, with body language there is no right or wrong, it's just weak or strong. Be kind to yourself. You're not looking for judgement, just information to help you understand how to do it a little better next time. You want to make sure your body language is consistent with what you want to communicate.

Challenge 4B: Practice your power pose.

For extra credit, you're going to spend two minutes at the beginning of each day practicing your power pose. The idea is to teach your body how to assume a confident position instinctively so you can increase your energy. Human beings have so much potential to move through the day with positive energy, and you can develop this ability through daily practice. So go ahead. Give it a try. Two minutes may seem like a long time at first, but it's a small price to pay for a lifetime of greater confidence and energy.

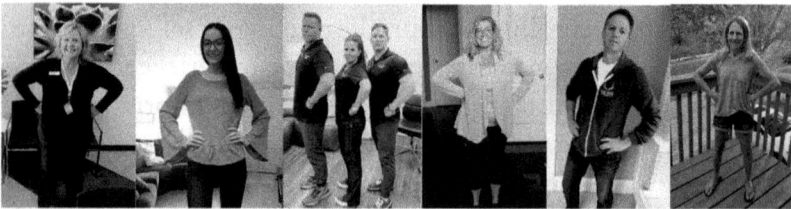

Expert Interview: Real World Virtual Exams with Dr. Brian Harris

Dr. Brian Harris, a self-professed dental nerd, has always felt a drive to bring cutting-edge technology into his dental business. Years ago he began incorporating virtual consults into his business model, and after performing over 4,000 consultations remotely he has some sage advice for anyone who is looking at expanding their virtual sales presence.

While tinkering with his technological approach, Harris made a pivotal discovery: the sales cycle in dentistry is broken. The traditional sales flow goes something like this: lead > phone call > show up > connect > discuss options > present treatment > talk money > discuss with spouse. The sales cycle is drawn-out with plenty of holes for a lead to fall through, from the office being closed when they phone to discovering at the in-person appointment that the price point is too high. Using this system, the ultimate close rates are somewhere near 30%. Dr. Harris knew that there had to be a more efficient way to connect with his clients.

Through virtual improvements, Harris eventually shortened the traditional sales cycle to this simplified version: lead > virtual consult > dental chair > acceptance. He advocates for capturing leads through a virtual landing page, securing client names, phone numbers, and other relevant data before the client ever sets foot in your office. This data is the key to marketing to each lead successfully. The new process allowed Harris to ultimately achieve sales conversion rates of 87%.

"When you have a prospect in the chair that you captured virtually, it's just like when you get a referral from one of your top clients," Harris explained. "You know they are already sold, they already trust you, they already know about pricing. Virtual allows you to achieve that level of confidence."

For Harris, the success of virtual consults is not in the personalized Zoom meeting. He feels that this individualized model is an inefficient use of his time. Instead, Harris promotes an asynchronous model, where information between business and client is exchanged back and forth without a formal virtual presentation. Asynchronous exchange allows Harris to train a sales assistant to offer information about his services, including price points. He believes that quoting pricing is a major factor in gaining client trust through transparency.

"I would like to invite innovators everywhere to change your process," Harris challenged. "Give yourself permission to reevaluate everything without judgement."

Harris' 5 Secrets to Successfully Use Virtual Consults to Grow Your Practice

1. **Create an Experience** so your clients know who to trust. *The Go-Giver* by John David Mann and Bob Burg is a great place to start. This book teaches you how to serve people without devaluing what you do.

2. Use **Social Proof** to create a personal brand and highlight what you love to do. For businesses, social media has become social proof, with real-life clients sharing their experience about your business.

3. **Less is More** in the virtual experience. Keep your interactions quick, between 5 and 7 minutes. Simplify and talk to people on their level because people like to buy from people.

4. **Create a Buzz** around your virtual transition. Place the news front and center on your website, put up a sign in your office, or put out a press release. You already have a following of people who trust you, so spread the word to take your audience up the service ladder.

5. **Involve your Specialist!** As you network with businesses that provide services adjacent to yours, bring these connections into the virtual experience. This type of networking will do wonders for your referrals as you share clients.

Stop! Don't Get overwhelmed.

I know there are some of you doctors and TCs who are eating this up and can't wait to practice these principles in your own practice. I know there are others who are in a place in their practices and personal lives and where incorporating these changes is not where you need to focus right now. I get that. That's called life. Be gracious with yourself.

If you are feeling the overwhelm, flip back to the end of the book to learn about **My Virtual Start**. Our Virtual Patient Acquisition services may be the perfect fit for the needs of your practice.

5

Words that tell and words that sell

I have a two-day training program where I visit offices and consult with business owners on how to create a better work environment. The first day is an observation day where I go in and watch the flow of the office and the body language of the team to better pinpoint areas we can improve. Of course, I don't announce to the staff that I am going to be watching their body language, otherwise they would be self-conscious and walk around like stiffs and I wouldn't get anywhere.

If you could observe your business from the outside, how would you describe the tone of your office? Is there a we're-all-in-this-together kind of vibe, or is it more like the Jets and the Sharks with the front office and the back office? The work environment is a major part of the lives of every member of the team. When you are spending a full eight hours a day together, most days you see more of each other than you see your family. If the tone of your office isn't one of collaboration, how do you change it? The answer is in your culture. When you change your culture, you change the tone.

The way to remove a culture of competition inside your office is to remove the struggle to compete with other businesses outside the office. As a business owner or team lead, you need to remove the scarcity mentality from your own mind. You want to develop a tone like Apple has. With the Apple mindset, the only competition is itself and everything else is just a PC. I have a client with an orthodontic business and you can literally see another orthodontist office from his front door. He could choose to let this close competition get into his head, but it would be the death of his relationships and his culture. Instead, he has developed a culture in his office that there is no outside competition. He has separated himself from the struggle to compete and focused instead on building a better team.

Some offices have developed a culture of 'I don't know.' In this section, we're going to be studying impactful and profound words. Some words trigger something deep inside of us. 'I don't know' is one of these deep-seated phrases, but for all the wrong reasons.

For the ladies who are reading this, think about how you feel when you come home after a hard day and ask your spouse or boyfriend what they want for dinner and they shrug and say, "I don't know." On a scale of one to ten, how sexy is that? Or when you ask what they want to do this weekend, and they say, "I don't know." It's the polar opposite of a turn on. I know that none of the ladies reading this are thinking that they just want to come home and ravish their husband's body because he doesn't know anything. I tell guys all the time, if you want to be wanted, stop using 'I don't know.'

If you want to stop your brain from processing anything, 'I don't know' is the phrase to do it. It simply shuts the thought process down. It also throws responsibility on the other person. I knew of one owner whose team would write down their questions on sticky notes throughout the day and stick them on his office door. At the end of each day, his team would go home and he would stay behind to answer all of their questions. That is not what we are going for.

The next time you hear, "I don't know," use this magic phrase: "I know you don't know. But if you did know, what would the answer be?" When you use these words, the other person will freeze. Their free pass to stop thinking will suddenly evaporate. Their ears might smoke or their eyes might roll in the back of their head. But then, they'll answer you. The answer will likely begin with, "I don't know, how about …" and they will give an answer. It might not be a good answer, but it will get their wheels turning again and get them in the habit of thinking for themselves.

Words are important! There are certain words that act as words of power, impacting us in unexpected ways. Countering "I don't know" with "I know you don't know, but if you did know, what would the answer be?" will shift the entire conversation. We focused on body language in the last chapter, which makes up 55% of how people communicate. Now we're going to focus on the other 45%, which includes word choice and tone of voice.

Though the words we speak make up only 7% of what we are trying to say, it's a huge part of what most people hear. As we choose our words with care, we will have more clarity and impact in our conversations.

The most important word in any language

> "A person's name is to that person the sweetest and most important sound in any language."
>
> -Dale Carnegie

When we are talking about words that are important and impactful, a person's own name is at the very top of the list. This one word represents a lifetime of connection and relationships. Using a potential buyer's name, and pronouncing it correctly, will make all the difference when it comes to personal connection.

Take it from a guy with the name Dino Watt, names are important. You can be standing in the middle of a buzzing crowd of a hundred people, and if someone uses your name, your mind lights up and you can hear it. Many people are sensitive about their name if it's unique or tricky to pronounce. But getting that name right is going to build rapport and help your client feel important.

When you are talking to a client, ask for their name early and use it repetitively. Jim Kwik, a memorization guru who works with big-name celebrities, advocates using a person's name three times within the first 30 seconds to 3 minutes of meeting them. As you speak their name aloud repeatedly, it will help that name become solid in your mind and you'll have a much higher chance of remembering the name later on.

Whenever I am working with a potential buyer, I keep their name right in front of me. Before I reveal anything new to that client, I intentionally use their name. In our example with Hannah, I use her name right before I reveal how much the treatment is going to cost her. I use it again before I send over the sales contract. In your sales presentation, any time you open a new door you will want to re-establish a personal connection by using their name. Use it at the beginning and at the end of the conversation.

You can also use your clients' names in the emails that you send, not just at the beginning but throughout the text. Just as you insert an autofill in the email's greeting, you can insert the name into the body of the text and personalize it even more. Most of your readers are going to recognize that it's an auto-filled email, but they will also be much more likely to read it and resonate with it if they see their name in the body.

When you come across a difficult name, ask for the pronunciation. Ask how to spell the name if that is helpful. For those readers who are coming across me for the first time, my name is Dino Watt, pronounced 'Dee-no,' not 'Die-no.' I can tell you from personal experience how frustrating it is to have people assume they know how to pronounce your name. It's also okay to ask if you have been pronouncing the name correctly, even if it's been a long time.

I have a client with an office manager whose first name is spelled Xaymara. Many of the people in the office call her by the nickname "Zimey." When I first met Xaymara, I told her she had a great, unique name. I asked her if I could call her Zimey and she said, "Sure," and she raised one of her shoulders! I was able to read what she was communicating and made the effort to understand how to pronounce the name. Now whenever I see her I use her full name and I can see in her eyes how she appreciates the effort.

Using another person's name is vital to connection. Here's one silly trick that you can use as an ice breaker when you forget someone's name. When I am having trouble remembering, I will ask the person, "What was your name?" They will respond with their first name, and then you can reply with, "Oh, of course I know your first name Becky, I was trying to remember your last name." It's a great little ice breaker that opens up that communication while helping them feel important at the same time.

RADAR WORDS

Throughout the sales conversation, there are some words that should be on your radar. As you listen for these words from your clients and use these words conscientiously, they will provide you with an opportunity to influence the situation. These words can set off a bell in your head and give you an idea of where to steer the conversation next.

Because

A Harvard study examined the persuasiveness of words and found the word 'because' to be extremely compelling. The researcher asked students to cut into a long line of people waiting to use a copy machine. The students used different excuses to justify jumping in line. The students who asked to cut in line using a simple, "Excuse me" were 60% successful. However, when they paired their request with the word 'because,' their success rates jumped to 93%. Even paired with an obvious excuse, such as "Excuse me, may I use the copy machine because I have to make copies?," the word 'because' was effective.

The word 'because' triggers a cause-and-effect sequence in our brains. It helps us organize a flow of events and we are more likely to go along with that sequence. So as you present to prospective buyers, position the word 'because' into your conversation as much as possible.

"Because you are interested in getting your tooth fixed and because I have a team ready to go and because we can fit you into our schedule, would you be opposed to starting today?" Here I stacked a list of 'because' statements and paired them with a 'no' question, and the result is powerfully persuasive.

Earlier I mentioned Chris Voss, a seasoned FBI agent and one of the foremost hostage negotiators in the world. I want to refer back to his book *Never Split the Difference* because he talks about how this word will shift the direction of people's thoughts. The reticular activator within the brain, which is responsible for our actions, is triggered by this word. If you want to motivate people to act, use 'because' when you are listing the reasons why they should buy. It builds up the evidence in their mind that they are making a great decision and going forward will be the natural progression of their thoughts.

Here are some examples:

- Because we value your time and because we are all concerned about exposure to illness and because we have the systems in place, would you be opposed to holding your exam virtually?
- Because I know you like to play your video game and because we have a rule about doing your homework before screen time and because dinner will be ready in about an hour, is now a good time to start your homework?

- Because we have the technology and because we have some availability this afternoon and because we can take the necessary steps to get you started through an online appointment, would you be opposed to having that consultation today?

When you use 'because' phrases, especially when you stack a list of these phrases together, you are building evidence. You are projecting credibility and professionalism. If you go into these virtual interactions with an attitude of, "Welp, I sure hope this technology works, you're our guinea pig," the client will pick up on that. You are a professional, so act like it. 'Because' phrases will go a long way in guiding your clients to participate in virtual presentations and interactions.

Stop naming the price! (i.e. leaving money on the table)

Would you like to make more money now, rather than later? I hope so. Money today is worth more than money in the future. However, many of you are leaving good money on the table by telling people how much of theirs you want. If you tell someone you expect a $500 down payment, you now set the bar at $500. This is a mistake. You never know how much money they have saved or are prepared to put down. It's not your job to tell them how much you want. It's your job to ask them how much they have to give you.

When you ask the client how much they were planning on putting down, it does a few crucial things:

- It gives them the opportunity to choose, and that gives them a feeling of being in control
- It establishes the assumption that they are going to put some money down
- You now know their starting point, rather than having shared your ending point

If you want more money as a down payment, ask the question, "So, how much money were you planning on putting down, or would you rather pay it off in full for a discount?" Then you let them answer.

If they say, "Well, I have about $1000 saved up for this, is that okay?" Well yes, that is okay. Simply by asking for the down payment that way, you just collected $500 more than what you would have asked. And yes, you should ask that to everyone, no matter what you believe your demographic is.

When I worked at Nordstrom, I was trained repeatedly that you never know what people value and will save their money for. Someone might come in wearing generic clothes with their hair not done and not looking like they had money, yet be perfectly willing to pay $500 for a pair of shoes.

Let me make this clear: You have no business stopping them from giving you as much money as they want.

If you have built your case as to why they should see your service as an incredible value, then don't cheapen it by undercutting your ask.

I cannot tell you how many clients and event attendees I have shared this with, only to have them reach out to me afterwards and tell me how much more money, on average they are getting as a down payment because they no longer set the bar and ask the question, "So, how much money were you planning on putting down, or would you rather pay it off in full for a discount?"

Okay, I know some of you are reading this and going out of your mind, even saying out loud something like, "But what if they say, 'Nothing' or '$100,' and you need more down to make it work?"

I hear you and I've got you covered.

If they do come back with a number you are not comfortable with, simply say, "That's great. We appreciate that. Most of our clients want to make sure they can keep that monthly payment down as low as possible so we like to see at least a $500 down payment. Is that the best you can do for a down payment?"

To see how to use this in a conversation, watch the bonus video at https://dinowatt.com/mve-bonus/.

> ## VIRTUAL REALITY
>
> Are you the first to disclose the price in your sales presentation? If so, start making the change of asking your clients, "How much were you wanting to put down as your down payment?" It's a simple shift that translates directly into more money in your bank account.

Is that the best you can do?

Do you want a better table at the restaurant? How about a later checkout at the hotel? Maybe a bigger discount on that dress? What about even a better "goodbye" from a loved one?

Years ago a mentor of mine, Ron LeGrand, taught me to get in the habit of saying the phrase, "Is that the best you can do?" as often as I can. His contention was that by using this phrase more often, your odds of receiving more in your life go up naturally.

Most of us don't even know what we really want in life so we sure as heck don't ask for more when we receive the "usual." This is a great way to politely ask the person you are dealing with if there is more available to you. Tone is everything when using this phrase. You don't want to sound demanding or forceful, instead use the tone of someone making a request.

I can tell you I have gotten everything from a free dessert at a restaurant to a 4 p.m. check-out time at a hotel. It works. This phrase can open the door to so many opportunities if you learn to use it, not just when closing clients but in all areas of your life. It is amazing the amount of money people are willing to offer when you allow them to name the payment first. Let's focus a little more on this phrase and what it can do for your closing conversations.

Anna: Alright Mike, Dr. Ivan says that you are a great candidate for Invisalign and that we can help you with your chewing concerns and give you that great smile you've been dreaming of. That's pretty awesome. Would you be opposed if I actually went through some of the investment for the Invisalign?

Mike: No, I'm not opposed.

Anna: Okay, great. I know we talked over our virtual chat and I gave you our price range for Invisalign, so you know that treatments range in price from anywhere between $4000 and $9000. The good news is that the model you fell in love with is not in that super high range, your total investment is only $6800. However, because of your insurance, your out-the-door investment is only $5800.

Mike: Okay, that's not too bad.

Anna: Yeah, I'm glad we can get you all set with that. Can I ask you, how much were you planning on putting as a down payment or were you planning on paying in full?

Mike: I think my first down payment can be about $500.

Anna: Oh, wow. You've thought about this and you've saved some money up. That's really impressive because I know it's challenging to be out on your own as a young adult. That's great. Now you know that the more you pay in the down payment the lower your monthly payments are going to be. Right now with $500 down, you're looking at just about $220 a month. Is that the best you can do on that down payment?

Mike: I could probably squeeze to about $750.

Anna: Great, congratulations, that's great that you have that money saved. That would get your monthly payment down to just over $210 a month. Now, just curious, because I love to help people get that monthly payment as low as we possibly can, is that the best you can do?

Mike: If I could get the monthly payment down to closer to $200 that would really benefit me. I'm getting a tax return and other things happening in my life, so I could probably do $1000.

Anna: Okay, $1000 would make your monthly payment right at $200.

Mike: Okay. That would be okay.

Anna: Great! I'm so glad we'll be able to do that for you. I'm so excited for you to start the treatment process. We actually have an opening in a few minutes for you to get your first scan, or we have some slots on Tuesday afternoon. Which would you prefer?

You can see in the conversation above that Anna actually used 'Is that the best you can do?' twice. It prompted Mike to consider other options and agree to a larger down payment. Don't be afraid to use it more than once if you feel it would help. And don't be attached to the answer, either. If they can't budge, they'll tell you it *is* the best they can do. You're not offending people; you're helping them get to the best payment option by asking them to reconsider what they can do.

One thing to remember here: If you are using 'Is that the best you can do,' you better believe some of your clients are going to use it back on you when it comes to pricing. You can anticipate that. And you have every right to say, "Yes, that is the best we can do." There is no guarantee that this phrase will work but it never hurts to ask, and most of your clients won't think to ask it back to you.

When someone says they only have 45 minutes, ask if that's the best they can do. If they say they can only do mornings, ask if that's the best they can do. When you are at the front desk of a hotel, ask if that's the best they can do. This phrase can be a secret weapon to have on your side during any type of negotiation.

For a video training on how to use "Is that the best you can do?," go to https://dinowatt.com/mve-bonus/.

Got it! Nevertheless

This phrase works like a dream whenever you want to be assertive and say 'No' to someone. It could be a client or an employee or a kid who has pitched you an idea and are pressing for a 'Yes' answer. Maybe they have even used 'because' on you and stacked the benefits, but you want to say 'No.'

'Got it! Nevertheless' is a phrase that lets the other person know that you heard them and understand their point. However, it is an answer that does not hinge on your having to argue back. The conversation might look something like this:

"Mom, I want to go out with my friends this weekend because I have been so good with my phone usage and my homework."

"Got it! Nevertheless, the answer is no."

This is the phrase you need for the guy who is pushing for a discount. It's the phrase you need for the woman who wants special treatment. 'Got it! Nevertheless' is a powerful communication phrase that will stop an argument in its tracks. It allows others to know you heard them, which is what every person on the planet wants, but also allows you to firmly close the discussion.

I agree

As you conduct your sales conversation, people are going to come up with all sorts of objections. Even if you have a really tight vetting process and only qualified buyers attend your presentations, objections often arise. You'll hear people say they need to talk to their spouse. You'll hear people say they need to sleep on it. You'll hear people say they need to consult with an astrologer. Here are a few insights into how I handle objections.

First, let me share with you some wisdom my once-boss Al taught me: People can lie to you and still go to heaven. People lie all the time, and it doesn't mean that they are evil or nefarious.

It often means they don't know what to say. Or they are embarrassed that the real answer is, "I don't trust myself."

As you ask for the sale and you get an objection like "I need to talk to my spouse" even though you know that all of the decision makers should already be on the call, don't get hung up on the discrepancy. Instead, agree with the person.

- I agree. Getting on the same page with your spouse is important. May I ask you a question? Did your spouse know we were talking today? Okay, great. So since they knew we would be having this discussion, what would they say if they were here?
- Man, I agree. Getting the straight smile you want can be expensive. It is definitely an investment, and I think it's one you are going to be happy with for the rest of your life.

When you hear those objections come along, be quick to agree with your clients. Validate their concerns, hear them out, and the move on.

I can see why you would say that ... It's unexpected

If you don't want to agree with someone or want to try a different angle, then use this little gem from a mentor of mine, Michael Bernoff. He is a master communicator and wrote a great book called *Average Sucks*.

If/when someone says, "Well that is just too darn expensive." Simply reply with, "I can see why you would say that." This way you acknowledge what they are saying but avoid agreeing with them.

Then follow up with the truthful, "It's actually not expensive, but it is unexpected."

The fact of the matter is that they are reacting to the unexpected nature of the price. They have no reference for what the investment or cost is, so they respond with a price objection instead of what it really is — a convenience objection.

VIRTUAL REALITY

How do you feel when people agree with you?
How do you feel when they disagree?

Decided and the -ly words

Have you ever had someone tell you they have "decided" on something? Well, this is for them.

"We've decided to wait until the first of the year because of our insurance". "We've decided to wait until the end of summer". "We've decided to hold off until COVID blows over".

For many, when you hear this word, it triggers something in you. You can easily think that 'Decided' indicates the thought process is over and done. The conversation is over. The client has cut off all other options and burned their ships. They are decided, right? Except they really aren't.

When was the last time you 'decided' to do something? You were decided and mentally committed. Except that a few days, weeks, or even minutes later you changed your mind. Maybe you had decided to get back to the gym, decided to lose the weight and get six pack abs, and then just a few days later (sometimes moments later) you changed your mind. Something caused you to go from a decision being made to the complete opposite action being taken. Maybe some other opportunity came up, or maybe it is just the reality of the 5 a.m. alarm and a bowl of ice cream. Whether it's getting a new hobby, picking up an instrument, or learning something challenging, we often decide on things and then shift gears.

However, when we hear this word 'decided,' we have a mental blind spot for its real meaning. We look at this word like it's inevitable. We think of it like gravity, as if it is the final word

127

and there's nothing else that can be done. Not true! 'Decided' indicates opportunity. It indicates that the person has given the purchase serious thought and may be open to persuasion. Don't turn off the conversation when a client uses this word, it is not a death sentence to closing the sale.

I view 'decided' as an **open-door word**. It indicates to me that the door is still open and there is wiggle room for negotiation and a different outcome. This means I am going to try a new angle or back up in the conversation and see how I can possibly change it around.

Speaking of "possibly", let's look at another category of word that means the door is still open. Words that end in "LY".

When someone uses a "ly" word it doesn't mean the conversation is over, it only means that much of the time they act, believe or choose something...but not always.

"Ly' words include the words: typically, usually, normally, basically, mostly, and supposedly. Train your ears to hear them, because they can be the beginning of a conversation, not the end as you have been led to believe.

When someone uses a "ly" word it doesn't mean the conversation is over, it only means that much of the time they act, believe or choose something...but not always.

Words like decidedly, typically, usually, normally, basically, mostly, and supposedly are all, temporary statements that are your invitation to change your approach, get clarification and overcome an objection.

You'll hear phrases like 'Typically I don't buy without my husband' or 'Normally I don't buy the same day.' These words indicate that there is a possibility of another option. I can't guarantee that you'll be able to change a client's mind when they are using these words, but you will often find wiggle room if you continue to pursue the sale.

Maybe 99% of other offices out there would stop at 'decided,' but I want this word to trigger an alert in your mind to continue the conversation. When you hear 'decided' or one of the '-ly' words, try responding with some 'because' phrases and see if you can stack enough evidence to change the direction of the conversation.

SAY THIS, NOT THAT

Some words naturally resonate with people and have a positive connotation. Other words evoke a negative psychological response. As you fine-tune the words you use you can smooth the way for lasting relationships. Let's talk about words that rile people up and some good alternatives that will set them at ease.

Problem (use Challenge or Opportunity instead)

You could say, "Dude, my mother-in-law is such a problem." The word 'problem' has a terribly negative feel to it. It's almost like a brick wall, shutting down any hope of things being better. Problems are heavy, they are serious. When you use, "My mother-in-law is a real challenge," you are more open to change. A challenge is something you can work with and get over. A challenge is an opportunity to do things differently.

Contract (use Agreement instead)

When you hear the word 'contract' it does not exactly conjure feelings of freedom and flexibility. Instead, you think about the cable contract or the cell phone contract. It's the feeling of being locked into a payment and trapped under a contract. Agreement, however, indicates a mutually beneficial relationship.

Signature (use Autograph or Approval instead)

From the time we are very young, we are taught that signatures are serious business. Getting that field trip permission was a big deal. We equate 'signing' and 'signatures' with the heaviness of a contract. Instead, say "Can I get your autograph?" People love to give out autographs. It's more fun and much more personal. "Can I get your approval?" is also a good neutral phrase to use instead of signature.

Just (use Simply instead)

If a client asks you how much time something is going to take, avoid saying, "Just 15 minutes." The word 'just' lessens the importance of the conversation, presentation, or fitting you are trying to arrange. If they are mentally debating whether or not to fit something into their life, you don't want to lessen its importance. Instead, use the word 'simply.' Something like, "This important step will simply take 15 minutes," will help the client understand its value.

But (use And instead)

The word 'but' has a contradictory feel to it. When you use 'but' in a sentence, it works to negate everything you have said up to that point. When I work with couples to strengthen their relationships, I hear a lot of 'buts.' The line usually goes something like this, "My spouse is the greatest person in the world, but ..." and then they unload with complaints that contradict their spouse being the actual greatest person in the world. Because 'but' tends to negate everything that was said before, it leaves a mixed message. Instead, simply say what you want to say. No need to try to soften it or contradict it with a 'but.'

Honestly or Truthfully

These are two words that you want to completely avoid using, especially in the middle of a conversation. If a client asks, "Do you own a vacation home?" and you begin your answer with 'honestly,' they will wonder about the integrity of the conversation before you used that word. If you have to use 'truthfully' to express yourself, it stands to reason that you were not being truthful before.

Patient (use Client instead)

This one goes out to all of my doctor friends. For any of you in the medical industry, try not to use 'patient.' When you hear the word 'patient' (and especially when you are called one), it brings to mind someone who is broken. A patient needs fixing. A patient is sick. On the other hand, clients are empowered. Clients make agreements and build long-term relationships.

Guarantee (use Warranty instead)

Often clients will ask if you guarantee your work. While guarantees are nice, they are also an invitation for people who will never be satisfied to take advantage of you. Offer a warranty instead for your clients to have peace of mind during the years ahead. Something like, "If your teeth ever shift during the next decade, we'll take care of it for a small monthly fee."

Discount (use Value, Promotion or Scholarship instead)

You never want to discount your product or service if you can avoid it. Instead, you can add value to your package, something low cost to you but that will be a high-value addition to your client. The term 'discount' cheapens whatever you are selling. When you run a sale, call it a promotion. Rather than discounting the price, offer a scholarship to help cover the cost. While a discount cheapens the service, a scholarship elevates it.

Buy (use Purchase, Invest or Enroll instead)

When you are discussing money with a client, you'll want to steer clear of words that evoke sacrifice. Words like buy, price, cost and fee have a negative, painful ring to them. Instead, talk about a purchase, an investment or an enrollment.

When I'm having a conversation with someone and they ask how much a program costs, I respond with "If it's not the right fit for you it won't cost you anything." I present the program, and then they decide if it's a good investment or not. Investment helps people understand that they are paying not only for the service today, but that it will continue to provide benefits in the years to come.

Obviously

Do not use. Obviously, this word is condescending and makes people feel dumb.

Any Questions or Any Objections? (use Area of Concern instead)

What happens to adults when someone asks if we have any questions? Here's what happens: we all have a terrible, deer-in-the-headlights memory of our middle school years and the last thing we want to do is ask a question. And asking about any objections is a highly negative way to phrase it. Instead, ask a client what their area of concern is. It's also helpful to be specific about what you want to discuss. For instance: What concerns do you have about the investment? What questions do you have about the warranty?

Hope (use Know instead)

When you work with a prospective client, don't use hope. You are a professional, and that prospect wants to be able to lean on your confidence and experience. They don't want to hear how you hope everything works out. Say, "We know you will love everything about your experience with us."

Suggest (use Prescribe or Diagnose instead)

Have you ever consulted with a doctor who acts indecisive? The doctor might take a look at you and sort of shrug and tell you that it's not really a big deal, that you could get surgery or not? It would make you feel like a fake or a hypochondriac. Instead, you want a doctor who takes charge, who takes your concern seriously and lines out the course of action to get things resolved. In your business, don't suggest. Diagnose. Prescribe. People are coming to you for your expertise, so take control of the situation and line out a plan to begin the service or program.

> ## VIRTUAL REALITY
>
> Which of these words are you most guilty of using?
> If you use one or many of them chronically, write the word along with its replacement on an index card and hang it near your workspace.

Paralinguistics

Now that we've covered radar words and learned how to choose impactful words, let's take a look at the power of your voice. Here we are dealing with paralinguistic speech, not the words you say but the way that you say them. Vocal tone makes up 35% of the message you communicate with others. Your voice is a powerful asset, and you can find-tune it to serve you better.

Tone can change your perception of someone. It indicates levels of confidence and capability. As you are selling virtually, you will want to be sure that you sound pleasant to others' ears, both onscreen and on the phone.

Whenever I think about paralinguistics, I think about Kathy Ireland. She started out as a supermodel and actress and eventually became a business mogul with a company worth $2 billion. Now, if you have ever heard Kathy Ireland speak during the height of her acting career in the 1980s, you will know that this woman had a powerful, remarkably high-pitched voice. During this time she worked with a coach who advised her to bring down her voice so people would take her more seriously. As Ireland's career progressed through the following decades, she trained her voice to drop lower and the difference you can hear is incredible. If you feel like your voice is something you are stuck with and cannot develop or change, do a search for Kathy Ireland and watch her progression from the 1980s into the 2010s.

Watch the video of the evolution of Kathy Ireland's voice at www.dinowatt.com/mve-bonus

Inflection

You'll want to avoid monotone speech and use intonation to add life to your conversation. One way of doing this is to smile as you speak or use your eyebrows to add expression if that works for you. This engages your energy levels and can bring your tone gently up and down. When you are closing with a client, you'll want to be sure not to drop your tone when you make the ask. As you request that price, be sure to maintain a steady tone.

Pitch

Pitch refers to the rate of the vibrations in your voice, or how low or high the voice is. When we talk about vocal pitch, the goal is the late-night DJ voice. That soothing, competent sound helps others relax and feel taken care of. You'll find this comforting voice in your lower vocal ranges.

Rhythm

Your rhythm is your cadence; the flow of the language as you speak. When you are engaged in a conversation, the goal should be to match the rhythm of the other person. If they are a fast talker, you want to bring up your speed, or if they are a slower talker you will slow down to meet their flow. Done right, this mirroring is important because you will be matching the speed of their thoughts and they will feel more in sync with you. Just don't go overboard when you are matching a client's energy level, as this can sometimes feel false to the other person.

Timbre

Timbre refers to the quality of your voice, that something that makes your voice distinctly yours. You might think of it as the difference between the same note being played on a piano or on a guitar.

Volume

As an on-screen presenter, volume is going to play a huge part in your communication. You want to make sure your speech is clear, so if you are a softer speaker, building up to a more confident volume is essential. On the other hand, if your voice tends toward too much volume you want to focus on toning it down so as not to be overpowering. We'll dive deeper into volume later when we set the stage for virtual sales through a technical setup, including choosing the right microphone.

VIRTUAL REALITY

What feedback have you been given about your voice?
If you have concerns about your voice, it's never too late to take voice lessons or hire a speech professional to help.

You will win the day with words you say.

As you begin to practice using words with intent and tuning your voice, you can project confidence and clarity. I have one last piece of advice around words and paralinguistics. If you get just one take-away from this chapter, I want it to be this: Record your conversations. Record your initial reach-outs, your phone conversations, your sales presentations. Listen to your own voice from someone else's perspective. This is the game footage that you want to see so you can track your progress and discover areas of improvement. The more you watch, the more you will see so you can master your message. Avoid critiquing and excuse-making. As you view yourself gently but honestly, you will find things to work on. Remember, it is not about being right or wrong, but being weak or strong.

All of the information in this section of the book is to help you gain more rapport with the people you sit across from, both in your personal and professional life. These tools will help you give them more reasons to know, like and trust you.

People like people who are like them or who they want to be like. Read that sentence again. The number one subject in any person's mind at any time is themselves. Your opportunity here is to help them see more of them in you. That will create the know, like and trust factor more than anything else you can do. The more you can learn how to use these skills, the more people will want to connect with you because they will see themselves in you.

Challenge 5A: Write your referral or sales close invitation.

For this challenge it's time to put pen to paper and write out an invitation for referrals. Referrals are an integral part of business and this exercise will help you practice your referrals ask. If it makes more sense in your industry, you can write an appointment invitation or a close invitation instead. You've learned the power of the word 'because,' so we're going to use its persuasive power in the referral statement. I'll get you started with the following template, but you'll want to use this framework to craft your own, individualized invitation.

For a simple-to-use template of the "Because" statements, download the PDF at https://dinowatt.com/mve-bonus/.

Once you have your template ready, it's time to make a recording and practice using your power language in front of the camera. You know how to hold your body to communicate effectively, and now you'll have a message to match it!

Challenge 5B: Use a radar word.

Because we retain the knowledge we use and because you want to be intentional in your speech and because it's really fun, would you be opposed to using one of the radar words today? Try out one of these words to sell someone into doing something for you. Use 'Got it, nevertheless' or 'I agree' or 'Is that the best you can do?' You can give these phrases a try in the workplace or at home with your family. See for yourself what happens when you employ the radar words. It can be a game changer for the way you connect with your team, the way you connect with your kids, the way you do your life.

Expert Interview:
Real World Virtual Exams with SmileSnaps' Greg Pellegrom

In April of 2019, Greg Pellegrom took a massive leap. His fifteen years in the dental and orthodontics sales industry had led him to a frustrating and disillusioned place. He knew well the challenges doctors were facing as they tried to compete with direct-to-consumer options and a referral system that was drying up, sensing with every office he visited that the industry was changing. The traditional model was no longer bringing in a steady stream of patients, and no one else seemed to understand that the doctors needed another solution.

Then one day Pellegrom had an idea. He asked himself why practices were requiring people to come into the office just to get basic information? He realized that most potential clients are looking for a relatively simple set of answers. They want to know if they are a candidate, how much the procedure will cost, and how long it will take. And most of these people have a smartphone, the most powerful tool on the planet, in their pocket. Why not tap into the power of the smartphone to create a virtual consult experience outside of the practice?

He reached out to a childhood friend in the tech industry and then faced the daunting task of pitching his idea to his wife and kids. With their support, SmileSnap was born. Pellegrom is now experiencing the most rewarding time of his professional career. He describes the success of his business and the positive feedback from practices worldwide as absolutely exhilarating.

Though an estimated 70% of people in the United States could benefit from orthodontic treatment, the orthodontic industry currently treats roughly 1% of them. Pellegrom's goal is to help doctors reach the other 69% through convenience and transparency. The rising orthopedic clients are the children of 80 million Millennials, and these parents aren't looking for a traditional model.

With SmileSnap, office hours no longer prohibit connection. Patients can sign up on Christmas day or connect with a doctor during the Superbowl. It works in both urban and rural environments, connecting people when travel is prohibitive. SmileSnap gets people off of their couch and into the chair.

Designed as a customizable software widget, SmileSnap is embedded in the doctor's existing website. As prospective clients interact with the widget, they are prompted to fill out their contact information and instructed to take 5 dental selfies, initiating the smile assessment process. Their information is captured and sent to the doctor, who can perform a smile assessment in minutes from his or her device. Once these prospects receive individualized information about their case, they come into the office informed and excited to begin their treatment.

Contrary to popular belief, the practices that are embracing SmileSnap are not all owned by young doctors fresh out of dental school. Pellegrom's technology is improving the practices of doctors of all ages, because adopting new methods is not about being young, it's about having an innovative mindset. SmileSnap is easy to implement and has a very attractive price point. To learn more about Greg Pelleman and the exciting things he's doing to support the ortho and dental industries, visit SmileSnap.com.

6

Building the Case

"My name is Dino Watt and I'm the best in the world at what I do."

There it is. It's a pretty bold statement, but I honestly believe it. I also believe that you are the best in the world at what you do. If you don't believe that yet, it's time to get convicted and own who you are. Your clients deserve you to believe it, and your team deserves you to believe it.

As we learned with power poses in the body language section, conviction creates energy. When you show up in your workspace, you have a choice to make: you can embrace a higher energy, or you can be an energy suck. Both types of energy are contagious, and owners set the tone for everyone else in the business. If you are reading this as an entrepreneur or a risk taker, you'll want to take notice. Your energy is often the key to attracting others to work with you.

One simple way to up-level the energy in your organization is through the titles you use for different roles in the office. Innovative, unique names can transform the way we show up in the office. When I work with a client in the orthodontics world, I advocate moving away from old, worn-out titles like receptionist, assistant, marketing director, financial coordinator, office manager and salesperson. Instead, we use bold titles like Director of First Impressions, Smile Architect, Ambassador of Buzz, Money Magician, Secretary of Defense and Sales Ninja. Even on paper you can feel the powerful energy of these titles.

Disney is a company that knows the power of language and uses it to set the tone. That's why if you visit a Disney theme park you will interact with Cast Members, be referred to as a Guest, and ride on Attractions instead of rides. Disney has created a culture within their theme parks that is unparalleled anywhere else, in part because of the words they use to describe the experience.

In this section we're going to take this same energy of being the best in the world at what we do and apply it to the virtual sales experience. In recent decades, economies have been pivoting toward virtual interaction. Ever since the internet became reliable, inexpensive and global, the opportunity to do business at a distance has made a lot of sense. Cost savings alone offer great benefits: more virtual means less office space, less time on the road, less traffic on our streets, more time with our families.

So why has it taken so long for a virtual selling experience to take root? I have found that for many business owners, the biggest obstacle to embracing remote sales is the idea that it is impossible to create the same experience for your clients as you can in person. We have this mindset that the depth of connection and communication cannot be replicated when we are not sharing the same physical space.

We need to let go of that mindset. For most industries, the in-person experience is simply not *that* amazing. In-person means that people have to carve extra time out of their lives and travel to you — time they would have spent at work or with their families. Unless you are in a destination industry, most people are going to be content to work with you virtually. With a willingness to do things differently and some creativity, you can overcome the challenges of digital sales. In fact, I believe that it is possible to provide an even better experience for your potential clients virtually than you can in person.

Remember that as a businessperson who is embracing virtual sales, you are a leader in your industry. You are using innovative techniques to guide your clientele before, during, and after their virtual experience. And that begins with educating people about what is possible virtually. There are two ways to do this, and one of them gets results.

Which of these options most closely describes your current virtual invitation?

A. So, we're offering this thing you can do, which is virtual, like, you can just do this from home, you actually don't have to come in if you don't want to.

B. We have made a change in our business model using this great technology which will allow us to start your educational journey from the comfort of your own home.

Okay now, be honest. One of those sounds like an innovative business leader, and the other sounds like a tween trying to get a first date. Be the strong leader you are, trust yourself and your systems, and be confident as you invite people to attend your presentations virtually.

Build Up the Invitation

The goal for the virtual presentation is to have prospects that show up primed to be open and ready to receive your message. You can accomplish this by building up your invitation with clients who already have an appointment with you as well as with those who have put out their feelers for your business but have not signed up yet. We're going to create a plan for you to market to these clients — and we're going to do it completely digitally.

The time between the initial invitation and the appointment itself is space that I refer to as the sweet spot. It is an essential phase because it is when you are psychologically enrolling people to show up with you online. I'm a big fan of doing things that will shock people's shorts, because in our loud world, this is what gets results. You want them to remember who you are and what you are capable of delivering, and the sweet spot is the time to remind them.

You are likely used to reaching out to your prospects through email or voicemail, and those are still great, reliable methods. Now, let's take a look at the other creative and unique ways to contact people virtually.

Digital cards

One of my favorite ways to make an impression digitally is by sending an eCard. When I was teaching this Selling Through the Screen course live, I sent a digital card to all of my prospects to get them excited about the course. The card showed an animated hamburger and it read, 'I'm working my buns off to provide an amazing Selling Through the Screen experience for you. Unless you have a beef with making more money, we'll ketchup at the event.' Yes, I know it's silly. But you know what? It also makes an impression and usually produces a smile as well. It's the impression that you are going for. Your clients are getting marketed to by the hour. If you can stir an emotion, you have made an impression.

There are many eCard services that provide excellent service. My personal favorite is American Greeting Cards. They have hundreds of designs and you can customize them to be as outlandish or serious as you want, with celebrities like Dolly Parton or Shaquille O'Neal to help you do it. You can brand a digital card to make it look professional and polished, or even attach a monetary gift card. A subscription to American Greeting Cards costs about $50 a year and there is no limit on how many cards you can send.

One of my orthodontic clients initiated a new system for keeping his office safer during the pandemic. To reduce headcount inside the office, he asked his clients to wait in the parking lot until it was their turn and used a digital card to greet them in their car. The card featured a cartoon cow dressed up like a movie theater usher and read, 'Hi, I am your parking lot attendant. We are busy sanitizing and getting ready for your treatment. Please be patient until one of us comes out to get you.' The eCard was simple, personalized, and a fun way to greet and inform each client.

Another way to personalize email communications is to send a video using BombBomb. This is an internet tool that allows you to send short videos inside your emails. Often when I send a quick video using BombBomb, I get a whiteboard and write the person's name on the board and wave at them. Then the client receives a .gif in their email of me waving. You could also make a short video or flip-book tour of your office. You can send a quick video with a breakdown of the financials to a potential candidate. A video is simple, personalized, and gets people's attention.

Because they are visual, eCards and video messages are memorable. Try sending one to a potential client the night before your appointment for a much more unique reminder than a text message.

VIRTUAL REALITY

What is unique about your or your practice that you could communicate to your clients in an ecard? Revealing your favorite things fosters an environment of sharing and can be a great conversation-starter.

Mail-order gifts

If you have a few days between the invitation and the appointment, sending a small gift to your prospective client is going to increase the wow factor big time. These gifts can be personalized by drop-ship companies in advance, so you don't have to get stuck figuring out the details each time. There's a psychological reason why getting physical swag beforehand is going to make a huge impression on your clients.

Robert Cialdini is a leading researcher on how people are influenced and persuaded. His book *Influence: The Psychology of Persuasion* is considered the bible on guiding people, and both you and your marketing team should have a copy on hand. Cialdini teaches the Law of Reciprocity, the principle that if you give people a little something, they will give you something back. We human beings are wired to return favors and tend to respond positively when we receive a gift.

One case study of the Law of Reciprocity at work involved a group of monks from India. In order to support their spiritual work, these Hare Krishna monks often go to airports or other high-traffic areas and ask for donations. You may remember seeing them in their orange and yellow robes. Donations were stagnating until the monks made a change to their model: they began giving potential donors a small paper flower while making their pitch. One monk would hand the flower to a prospect, the prospect would take it and throw it away, and another monk would retrieve it from the trash to use again. But something was happening to these potential donors between the time they received the flower and the time they threw it away. The gift of the flower initiated a different response than the mere verbal request for a donation. As a result of those inexpensive, reusable flowers, the Hare Krishna donations skyrocketed. The Law of Reciprocity works because people tend to do unto others as they have done unto us. As the monks handed out those flowers, people gave of their spare change more freely. When we receive a gift, we are much more likely to give.

You can get the Law of Reciprocity working for you as well. When you don't have to maintain a physical space for sales, the coffee, bottled water and magazines are no longer necessary. You are selling virtually, so you can shift those marketing dollars to send out gifts beforehand. A cookie, a coffee mug or gift card will let your clients know you are thinking of them and will make a great impression.

One of my clients, an orthodontic office in Detroit, has set up an amazing model using the Law of Reciprocity. When someone comes in for their first consulting visit, there are two gifts waiting for them: one for the parents and another for the child. Of course, the office also offers exceptional service, and no amount of giving can take the place of an excellent product. However, the office has learned to use the principle of giving to guide those parents into a mindset where they have already made an exchange with the business and are primed to make exchanges in the future.

I recommend the company Banner Season to help you with your mail-order gifts. You can create different marketing campaigns and send all sorts of swag. I use Banner Season to send a brownie to my podcast guests after our time together. It's a great way to connect and thank them for their time and expertise. Another great direct-ship company is 3Dmail.

To make your giving the most effective, there are a couple of things to remember:

1. Great gifts are unexpected.

Your client is going to be expecting paperwork from you or a marketing brochure in the mail. They will not be expecting swag.

When you surprise someone with something unexpected, a neuro-alert goes off inside their brain. This signal conveys to them the importance of this moment, so they get excited and pay closer attention. The cognitive resources in their mind get hijacked and pulled into the current moment. Think back to the last time someone surprised you and you were thinking, "I can't believe they thought of me!" Because your attention is completely in the moment, your emotions are intensified. With a positive surprise comes happiness, joy, and positive feelings towards the person who surprised us, just as a negative surprise will lead to intense feelings of anger, despair and unhappiness. Create a plan that will capture those good-will emotions!

I have observed a strange phenomenon when I am in the market as a buyer. I experience a sense of irony when I make a major purchase like a car or an elective medical treatment and after I sign the contract they give me a T-shirt or a key chain. In my mind I'm thinking, "Wow, I just bought an $8,000 T-shirt." It doesn't make any sense to me that the seller would hand out the swag after I've signed the contract. It seems like an odd thing to do once it's a done deal. Instead, give your prospects the gift beforehand. Mail them that shirt. Send an iTunes gift card. They'll never be expecting it!

2. Great gifts are personalized.

There is nothing like a personalized gift to make a massive impression on your clients. When you send specialized swag before your presentation, it shows people that you care about them individually. They will sense that your clients mean more to you than just numbers and that you care enough about them to put forth effort.

I have a few pieces of Dino Watt swag that I love to give out when I do speaking appearances. Lately I've given out branded pens and these great little cell phone handles with my name on the band (the company that manufactures them is called Love Handles if you want to check it out). But what will connect you even more to people is to have your branded gear with *their* name on it. One dentist purchased toothbrush holders for his clients and had their first name etched in the metal. Not only does this gift have a personalized touch, but his clients are going to see it every single day.

I am a huge Donny Osmond fan. From the time I was a little kid who dreamed of being a performer, Donny was a hero to me, and I wanted to be just like him. Imagine my delight when I discovered that American Greetings has a birthday card featuring Donny Osmond. I can send out this card and Donny actually sings Happy Birthday to the receiver. It is so personalized that I can indicate the person's name and age and Donny will sing the name and the age.

If you are serving a local market, find a local vendor who can personalize and mail gifts for you. Or find a vendor on Etsy who is willing to create and ship what you need. Starbucks and M&M's have options that allow you to brand and personalize gift cards. Taking the time to make things personalized adds an entire new level of excitement and engagement.

3. Great gifts are meaningful.

This is the ultimate level of gift giving and provides a foundation for true connection. In his book, Cialdini tells the story of a real estate brokerage that was trying to woo a prospective investor. They tried traditional ways of getting this investor to meet with them and the meeting never happened. What ultimately grabbed the investor's attention was when the brokerage sent a picture of an art gallery that they knew he was passionate about. The solution wasn't expensive, but it was more challenging. To find out what is meaningful to your potential clients is the path to connection.

In our connected world, many of your clients will have a social media presence of some kind. You can figure out which sports team they root for or whether they like exotic teas through a quick Facebook or Instagram search. Sending something that strikes a meaningful chord with your clients makes an impression and gives you something to open with when you meet on screen.

The ultimate professional swag

Here's a tip that will help you establish your professionalism like nothing else. If you want to portray yourself as an expert, you need to write a book. Books provide credibility and establish you not just as a professional, but also as a teacher. You can write about the top questions everyone is asking about orthodontics.

You can write about investing in the real estate market. You can write your 10 best hints for budding entrepreneurs.

You don't have to be an amazing writer to produce a book. There are many ways to get your life work into print, and they can coincide with your natural talents and abilities. Since verbal communication comes most naturally for me, I typically launch new training in a classroom environment. However, even as I create and teach the course, I have tools in place to write the book to go with it. I take notes of my research, record my training, and use speech-to-text translators to create a working manuscript. Then I hire amazing editors to help me put all of my work together and ready to print.

Having your name on a book very quickly establishes your expertise, making your book a great gift to send out to prospective clients. You can even personalize it by including the recipient's name with your signature inside the cover. Giving your book as a gift is unexpected, can be personalized with your autograph, and will be meaningful to any clients who are seeking you out.

When you connect with clients before a sales presentation, you prime them for an incredible experience. eCards, personalized videos, or gift cards are a great way to do this electronically and there's nothing quite like a mailed gift that a client can hold in their hands to provide connection. When you are planning and implementing, don't overthink it. The gift does not have to be a production. Simple and done is better than well-planned.

As you sell through the screen, you can shift your marketing budget over from the in-person consumables to gifts that you send through mail or email. Your ability to reach out and connect with your potential clients in the real world before a presentation will bridge the virtual selling gap. They will recognize that your services are solid and that you can provide real value to their lives, which is going to go a long way during your sales presentation.

Build a Virtual Experience

When you are building a virtual sales experience, you get to actually produce that experience. You don't have to spend a lot of time or money getting everything to look just right. On the other hand, you definitely don't want to go into a sales presentation at the last minute, hoping that your computer is already set up with what you need to create a professional-looking, next-level video experience. Here are my best tips to look and sound the part during your video calls.

Lighting

If you want to get that really professional, clean look on camera, then great lighting is going to be your best friend. You may have noticed the lighting during the video challenges you have created thus far. In those videos did you look backlit, with bright light behind you so that your face is a dark silhouette? Was the lighting dim, making it difficult to see your face and hands? Getting the lighting right can make a big impression on your clients.

To get great lighting you'll want to invest in a ring light. A ring light is a halo-shaped light that illuminates the entire face. They come in several sizes, and the ones I see most often are a small cell phone light, an 8-inch diameter and a larger 18-inch diameter light. Any of these lights will help give you that clear, bright look. My recommendation for most people is to get a good 8-inch ring light.

Sound

Another huge aspect of the video sales experience is getting your sound right. Video sound is one of those things that you don't really notice when the sound is good, but it's completely distracting when the sound is bad. Cheap secretary headsets create a hollow sound. Many out-of-the-box computer microphones pick up a lot of ambient noise and sound like the person is in a wind tunnel or create an echo-chamber effect. You'll want to get a really good understanding of how your microphone stacks up before any sales presentation.

Getting a great microphone is going to help you in two ways: it will allow your client to hear your voice and see your body language. We talked before about how important it is that people can see both your face and your hands to engender trust. A good microphone will allow you to sit or stand farther away from your camera so a client can see your face and hands and still hear you.

A great option for a microphone is a USB microphone that will plug right into your computer, whether it's a Mac or a PC. Most of these models will automatically interface with your existing system and don't require any additional software. The microphone models that I know work well are the Blue Yeti or Blue Snowball.

Getting great sound is more important than visual effects. Sound is the best conveyor of your message through your words and your body language. With a great microphone you won't be tethered to your monitor. You'll be able stand a few feet away from your computer and express your energy through your movement and your hands, bringing your sales presentation to life.

Camera

As you set up your virtual office space I recommend at least one good webcam. You don't want to go overboard with a high-end camera that requires a video capture card, but you also don't want to stick with the generic camera that came with your computer.

My best pick for a great webcam is the Logitech C920. It's another great plug-and-play USB device that interfaces directly with your computer and offers a sharp picture. If you want something a little more professional, I also love my Canon M50. It's a mirrorless DSLR camera to get that really clean look.

The first time I presented the Selling Through the Screen challenge I had a bit of a live TV emergency. The indicator light on my webcam started blinking because the battery was dying right in the middle of my presentation. Luckily, I had my other webcam on hand, and it was easy to unplug the one that was running low, plug in the other one, and resume the presentation. When you are considering purchasing any of this equipment, from the lighting to the microphone to the camera, you want to think simple and effective. Plug-and-play USB models are going to allow you that flexibility.

Camera angles

In the early days of the quarantine when everything was shut down I watched a clip from The Tonight show. Because of the pandemic, celebrities were video calling into the show from their homes, giving it a more personal, home-video sort of feel. One of the guests was the one and only Hugh Jackman, and his video camera angle was so bad that I was looking up at his chin and up his nose.

Hugh Jackman and his wife,
Debbie on The Tonight Show with Jimmy Fallon

Here he was, this huge star of stage and screen, chatting with Jimmy Fallon with his camera featuring his kitchen ceiling. I'm not sharing this with you to be harsh, but rather to convey to you the importance of camera angles. It's okay that Hugh Jackman doesn't do camera angles. He's got people to take care of that. To be fair, he eventually figured it out and was able to get a better angle, but let's take a lesson from him and be aware of the direction the webcam is pointed.

To make things a little easier for you, I created a special camera angle scale that I have for your educational enrichment. One extreme is having the camera too high, so the focus is on your forehead, or what I call, "the Kardashian angle".

The other extreme is having the camera so low that you become all chins, or the Boomer angle.

The goal is to be somewhere in the middle.

To make it extra simple, just follow this graphic and all will be ok.

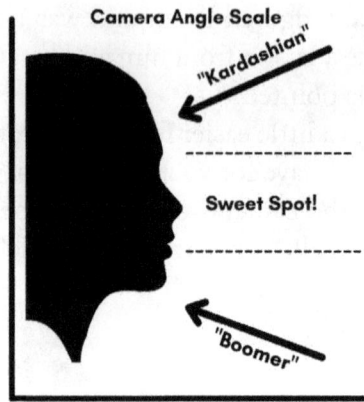

Camera Angle Scale
"Kardashian"
Sweet Spot!
"Boomer"

When you are setting up your camera, the sweet spot is to get the picture straight on and slightly above your eye level. Adjust your angle with your webcam turned on and then look into the lens of the camera. You want to make sure that your camera is angled just above your gaze, so you are looking up a bit, as if you are paying attention.

With your gaze angled upward, you psychologically convey a sense of respect to your audience. Subconsciously they will feel elevated and in control, which will help their concerns fade away. During a video call you might be tempted to use your keyboard to type in some data, bringing your gaze down. Choose instead to use a pen and paper to take notes and transcribe them later rather than typing while your client is talking. Your clients will see more of your gaze and won't get the feeling that your attention is divided.

You'll want to use good camera angles anytime you record yourself. When you are in doubt if your angle is too Kardashian or too Boomer, just look to see if the angle is flattering to you. It's good practice during personal video calls and especially important during professional calls.

I once taught an online training to a client who couldn't figure out how to adjust the angle of their webcam. The camera was recording from the bottom corner of their computer at this funky angle for the entire session. It was more difficult to connect with my client in an authentic way when I couldn't see their face. When you are setting up your camera, be aware of things that will make the experience less personal for your clients. We're trying to create an environment that will bridge the distance between us and make conversations feel as natural as possible.

Green screens

Filmmakers have been using green screens for over a century and using a green screen to project a backdrop is becoming more and more common in business. I love to use green screens. My green screen allows me to film quality videos whether I am working from my office, from home, or anywhere else.

There are two basic types of green screens. One is the large photographer's background that you are probably familiar with from films and weather reports. The other is called a pop-up green screen, a smaller version that comes with a stand similar to an art easel. Another version attaches to the back of your office chair. These pop-up green screens are the ones you want. They are green on one side and have blue on the other side, which comes in handy if you are going on-camera and find yourself wearing a green shirt. Another option is to paint the wall behind you green or to hang up a green sheet. The effect will be the same.

Green screens are being used so widely that most video conferencing platforms such as Zoom and GoToMeeting have green screen support. You can indicate within the platform that you have a green screen and then select from a variety of backgrounds. You can even create a background that is personalized with your name or logo or is an image of your actual office.

My go-to green screen is a pop-up that I can pull down and then it rolls back up. It allows me to record amazing, professional videos on a Saturday in front of my open bedroom closet in my bare feet. I can find a favorite background or use a different background in every video to keep my clients guessing.

To get a really polished look with a green screen you may have to play with your lighting. I usually have one ring light above me and another one off to my right to help with the green screen effect, otherwise there is some shadowing.

Sharing visuals

As you prepare to present on-screen, be sure to get to know your video platform or software so you can make the best use of visual effects. Visuals are memorable and will elevate your presentation in a big way. Let's say you want to show your potential client a picture of a Tesla Model S in deep blue metallic. You can use screen sharing to show the image on your computer screen. However, as you share your screen, the video of your face gets minimized and moved to the bottom of your client's computer screen. This minimization will get in the way of your eye contact, your body language, and can ultimately break the rapport that you were building.

There are programs that allow you to present the picture of the Tesla without losing your connection with the client. Here are a few open source platforms that will allow you to project an overlay of the object on top of your video image: Ecamm for MAC users (https://ecamm.com/), or OBS (https://obsproject.com/) and Streamyard (https://streamyard.com/) will work whether you have a MAC or a PC. The overlay effect will show you presenting the picture of the Tesla rather than being replaced by it. These tools allow you to maintain the face-to-face feel with your client while presenting a picture or report.

As you are researching video effects in preparation for your presentation, YouTube is going to be a great resource. You'll find up-to-date guides to help you create beautiful presentations. One of my favorite how-to videos is by Mike Koenigs. You can find Mikes great training on YouTube by searching "Mike Koenigs, 25 Strategies to make your Zoom Meetings Awesome"

There are so many great apps and widgets out there to help you with your visuals. You can create a setup as if you are an anchorman on a news report with a ticker-tape banner below you. You can cast the video image of another person onto the screen beside you. Be creative. Consider production and which visual effects are going to work best for you to take your conversations to the next level.

Your lighting, microphone, camera, angle, green screen and image sharing will impact the quality and professionalism of your sales presentation. I estimate that you can create a great teleconferencing setup for less than $300, but as demand for virtual workspace support increases, costs will likely fluctuate. The goal is to work with your technology beforehand so that the presentation has the feel and connection of a face-to-face conversation.

If you take the time to make the experience smooth and professional looking, you will have a leg up on others who simply turn on a zoom meeting with no real thought behind it and I promise your potential clients will notice the difference.

Build Case Studies

In all areas of your business, you want to build the case that you are the best at what you do. Curating a collection of great client reviews that you can share with potential clients will lend your business credibility like nothing else can. Though there are many types of social proof that your business is incredible, some are more effective than others. There is a hierarchy of good, better, and best when it comes to client reviews.

When a client posts a shoutout on social media after you have really wowed them, these posts are good. Great reviews on Google Ads are good, too. Even better is when a client provides you with a testimonial. The best social proof that will impact your clients the most is the case study. Though you do want to be tagged, tweeted about, and liked, the most important social proof to focus on is the case study.

The case study allows you to prompt your client to build your case for you. The case study begins with a detailed description of the customer's situation, the problem they were having, the process by which the problem was addressed, and the outcome. Case studies allow your client to speak to a broad audience, relating and connecting to more people. We explored the power of stories earlier, and we'll use that power again to resonate with more people during the case study.

When you record a case study on video, you can keep that documentation to bring up repeatedly. You can edit the story and isolate relevant pieces that you want to share. You can create a case study library for your business to help connect you with your prospects, whatever their situation.

When I am consulting with a business owner, I often ask them to tell me one transformational story. I want to know about a time when one of their clients had a really terrible or sad background story and through their business they were able to take this person to another place. I want to hear about how they transformed someone's life. You likely have a story just like this, or if you are new in the business, you will. This is the perfect example of a great case study.

When you film a case study, you have the option of telling the story yourself or asking the client to tell their story. You can guide them to say exactly what you want them to say, rather than making them guess. It's also a great idea to have case studies from a wide representation of people: people with tattoos, people with piercings, people with purple hair, young people and old people. The more variety you have in your case studies, the more likely your videos will resonate with many people.

Key Elements of a Great Case Study:

- Where the client was before
- What the client hoped to achieve, or their goal
- Why the client chose to work with you
- What was the client's experience like?
- What were the client's results?
- Would the client recommend the process?
- Allow the client to thank you!

Sample direct statement from the client:

"You should visit Luigi's Spaghetti Factory because …"

"You'd be missing out if you didn't use Brandon's Doggie Grooming because …"

These case studies will be invaluable. I want you to have them everywhere. They should have a prominent place on your web site and be part of your marketing campaigns. You can never have too many testimonials.

VIRTUAL REALITY

What specific type of case study do you think would draw in the most clients? Who do you know that you could ask to help you create this case study?

The truth is that your clients buy the sales experience. More than any other indicator, people buy based on what they experience during the sales process. If this were not the case, there is no way McDonald's would be this prolific. No one is fooled by their professions of quality or the beautiful pictures of their food;

everyone knows that McDonald's is terrible for you and what you get in your take-out bag is different from what you were being sold. But McDonald's has created a sales experience that draws people back in every time. McDonald's clients are loyal, even when they have a bad experience, and return over and over again.

While I'm not advocating that you use McDonald's as your business standard, I do want to encourage you to mirror their sales experience. If a great sales experience can build a loyal client base around mediocre fast food, imagine what it could do for your business. Build the case for your business through a phenomenal invitation, a great virtual experience, and a curated library of case studies to enhance the sales experience.

Challenge #6: Create Your Case Study.

For this challenge, I want you to create a case study for your business. You're going to think of your own transformational experience that you had with a client you served. You're going to make a recording of yourself telling that story in under three minutes.

Before you ask someone else to do something, you must first be willing to do it yourself. As you create your own case study, you will come to know the questions and challenges involved so you are ready to help your clientele create stellar case studies for you. They will better understand the importance of their testimonials and they will feel safer with the knowledge that you have been through that experience yourself.

You'll want to get your set-up in place with your camera, microphone, backdrop and lighting. Pay attention to your camera angle to make sure you don't look like a Boomer or a Kardashian. Remember that the beauty of the case study is that you can produce it yourself and get exactly the review you want. Here's an example of a recent case study that a client gave for me:

"Hi guys. Nickole Bradfield here. I've been in the orthodontic industry for over 30 years. About a month ago I decided to take a

course called Selling Through the Screen with Dino Watt. I got so much out of it and enjoyed it so much I decided to go on and take his more extended Blueprint course. A client of mine took the course as well and I'm with that client this week. Though we're only three weeks into the Blueprint course, the way that Dino structures this class, the way he assigns the homework and the projects that we do has allowed this client of mine to restructure their protocols, bringing them to this post–COVID high touch, high tech communication way of life that we're all getting used to. And I'm watching them have a record week and we are on par to have a record June and looking ahead at their July and August, those are going to follow suit. So for all those naysayers that said the orthodontic industry was going to be down, for those who said we'd be lucky if we're only down 25%, I'm gonna throw the BS leg on that. I suspect that if you take courses to improve yourself, you work hard to work digitally, and you do things like what Dino offers in the Selling Through the Screen Blueprint, you're going to blow that out of the water. So do yourself a favor, get in touch with Dino and be in the Blueprint."

You can create a template and walk people through the case study process. Make it your own and brand it to yourself. Guide your clients to create the content and then use the case study videos and documents to create testimonial stories for yourself. Start today and start with your own story of how you changed someone else's life.

Expert Interview: Real World Virtual Exams With Dental Monitoring's Brian Kleindienst

In 2020, the dental and orthodontic industries were blindsided by a massive, unprecedented lockdown due to the COVID-19 pandemic. Schedules were wiped clean, offices emptied and team members remained at home. The pandemic forced a world-wide change of paradigm and consumers will never go back to looking at economic exchange the same way. They have become more comfortable with virtual interaction, efficiency and reliability, and this is going to have a profound impact on the healthcare industry.

As telehealth becomes the new standard in medical care, a bold team of disruptors at Dental Monitoring wants to take the dental industry one step further. Their vision is not just about changing the venue of dental care through virtual teleconferencing. Instead, they are looking at completely revolutionizing the industry through the use of a personal dental monitoring device that can scan the patient's teeth and send information to the doctor in real-time. Through the use of artificial intelligence, these dental scanners are capable of providing even more micro-level precision than a doctor is capable of in-person.

"Dental Monitoring empowers both sides. It's a win for the office and the patient," explains Brian Kleindienst, Dental Monitoring's North America sales rep. "The doctor becomes the quarterback, able to program 180 clinical notifications such as liner fit, recession, or hygiene, depending what they are targeting. The doctor controls all of this."

With the help of their powerful analysis technology and innovative scanning device, Dental Monitoring is capable of tracking patients on a weekly basis, alleviating the need for manual check-ups or the arduous task of looking at photos one-by-one. "The last thing you need as a doctor is another job," Kleindienst points out. "That's why this is all automated. It's the perfect symphony between human interaction and machines. You can download all of the information, and then use the creativity and flexibility of your mind to get the best results possible."

The Dental Monitoring funnel begins with an initial scan of the patient to create a treatment protocol. With help of artificial intelligence, the program has the capability to create a smile prediction, morphing the patient's smile to what it will look like during and after treatment. This objecting reporting system will help your patients have a vision of what your practice can deliver, and help you fine-tune and streamline your processes.

The actual scanning device, called a Scan Box, is a hand-held frame that the patient can slide their smartphone into. A cheek retractor is attached to the frame to help the patient access those hard-to-reach teeth. With the help of a voice tutorial and a mirror, the patient adjusts their phone camera and their device captures the images automatically. The scanning process takes about two minutes and creates three high-quality scans for the AI to analyze and deliver to your office. The platform automatically sends each patient a push notification to remind them when it's time for a scan. The Scan Box device, coupled with Dental Monitoring technology, is like an insanely reliable clinical assistant, working 24/7 to serve your patients and help you stay relevant.

If you are looking to revolutionize your office, Dental Monitoring might be the right next step for you. To find out more about this immersive new platform that can put your practice in a different stratosphere, learn more at Dental-Monitoring.com.

7

Closing the Deal

Do you remember your first kiss? Whenever I ask this question, I get a mixed reaction. There are a few people who will get excited about it, and others are more like, "Meh. It wasn't that great."

My first kiss happened at an 8th grade dance. Her name was Angela Sandaval and she was my girlfriend, which meant we had held hands. My parents hadn't allowed me to go to dances until I was 14, so this was my very first dance and I was so excited. I had some dance moves that I was ready to show off, but we all know that when it comes to connecting with someone special, it's the slow dance that counts. So I was standing there against the wall of the gym with my buddies when I heard a slow song come on and things got serious. I went over and asked Angela to dance and we started doing the middle school shuffle, awkwardly swaying from side to side. I looked around and noticed that my buddies were all kissing the girls they were with. And they weren't just kissing, it was a bit more exotic than that, a bit more foreign, a little French action was going on around me. I had never kissed a girl before, and there I was, just swaying. It was a profound moment for me. I still remember the song; it was

Chris de Burgh's "Lady in Red." Well, I thought, everyone else is doing it. So without saying a word, I leaned in, and then she leaned in a little bit, and I thought, "I'm in." I was so excited.

Finally, we met in the middle and had a nice kiss. I was feeling pretty good about that, so I decided to go for it. All of the sudden our tongues started touching, and I remember thinking, "This is disgusting! Why would people do this?" I was thinking about the spit and the awkwardness of it, and we just kinda kept going with the song. It was a quick moment, but that moment changed everything.

After a while we separated and awkwardly looked around. The first thing that I noticed is that we were not alone in our dance space. There was a string of spit suspended in the air between us, sort of swaying to the rhythm. And I'm thinking, "That's not supposed to happen. That doesn't happen in the movies." I find a way to casually karate chop the air between us to break the strand of spit. Finally the song ended and we didn't say anything. Angela ran off to the quad with her girlfriend and I joined my buddies at the wall, standing a little taller.

It wasn't three minutes later that Angela's friend came back to get me. I was flying pretty high at this point. I swaggered confidently out to the quad, where Angela told me nine words: "We're moving too fast, we need to break up." That is the story of my very first kiss.

That moment is seared in my head all these years later — the song, the spit, the nine words. Do you have experiences that are seared in your head? The power of the moment, the energy of the space, the body language, the words. People are powerful! We have the power to effect change through our words, our movements, our communication.

I guess you could say that my first kiss with Angela Sandaval was less effective than it could have been. As a middle schooler, I had a lot to learn about relationships, communication, and connection. During the intervening years I've studied and practiced these elements intently because the same principles that help you build strong relationships also help you close sales. There's only one way for a business to grow, and it's through sales. Cash into the business produces growth. As a business owner, you have to know and own the sales process so your business can stay afloat.

You can have an amazing marketing program that draws many people to connect with your business, but if you can't close the deal, it's all for nothing. Salespeople have a ton of responsibility. They are responsible not just to keep the lights on at the office, but they also make sure that their teammates can pay the rent. It's an incredible position that carries with it incredible responsibility and opportunity.

I've supported my family for twenty years on my sales commission, and that's commission only with no safety net. It's risky. There is no guarantee. But I also get to write my own check every week, which is a powerful thing.

For business owners who hire a sales force, you can't ask others to do something you're not willing to do. That doesn't mean that you have to quit your position and join the sales team, but it does mean you should know what a good close looks like.

Closing Techniques

Using Urgency

One great closing tool is a time-based technique. When you utilize this method, you will inform your clients that you have a promotion or an increased value to offer them, but for a limited time only. If the client misses out on the time period you specified, they are no longer eligible for that promotion. With a time-based close you are using the clients' sense of urgency to help them take the next step.

The key to the time-based close is to be in integrity when you make the offer. If your potential client comes to you after the promotion window, they do not get the promotion. When you are staying in integrity, you will believe yourself when you describe the limited-time offer and the client will sense that. You present what you are willing to do and you stick with your own timeline of when the promotion is no longer valid.

This technique is especially useful if you have a client who is waffling about a start time. You can give them a bonus to encourage them to get going with your service. You could offer to match a client's down payment by 10% if they make that payment by the end of the day. If they really have to talk to their spouse or move some money around, this will give them a sense of urgency to get those tasks completed. When you use a time-bound approach, you will have people calling you five minutes before the day ends to send you money, so you'll want to be prepared for that.

Now, if the client calls the next day, it is imperative that you no longer honor that promotion. I know some of you reading this are going to think I'm a stickler, but hear me out. When I let a client know that they have missed out on the window of opportunity, they often tell how much they appreciate my integrity. It will not turn away a great client, but will often give them even more of a desire to work with you. They will understand that you honor your word.

Using Scarcity

When I was facilitating the live Selling Through the Screen challenge, I began with the goal of getting 50 people to attend my first challenge. After I met that goal, I bumped the goal up to 100 people. I wanted to affect the lives of 100 people. However, I do have a cap on how many people I can have in my virtual training room. I used the scarcity inherent in the cap to encourage people to sign up for the challenge.

When you are working with your clients during your close, you will also have inherent limitations on what your business can do. You will have a limited number of hours in the day. You have a limited amount of chairs in your office. You are affected by the new laws and limitations of Covid-19. You only have a few slots, so tell people you only have a few slots. Why? Because you do.

You can only physically do so much and you can use this scarcity to nudge the close.

Robert Cialdini, our persuasion guru, once went to the electronics store to buy a television. He had done his homework and knew what he wanted to buy. A salesman in a polo shirt came to help him out and told him two things: first, the television on display was the last one the store had in stock, and second, a woman had just called him to hold the TV for her to come pick up. This salesman had no idea who he was talking to. Of course, Cialdini is thinking, "This guy is using scarcity and urgency on me!" He decided to go ahead and purchase the television. However, he was also determined to go back to the store the next day.

As a salesperson, your job is to make sure that your potential clients do not feel the pain of regret. You want to guide them to get what they want, and that's why you use scarcity. It is a great tactic, but just like with urgency, you must be in integrity when you use scarcity. Cialdini knew that if he went back to the store and saw the same model of his television on the wall, that the salesman had been out of integrity. People don't like to be lied to.

The following day Cialdini walked into the store and sure enough, the space where his television had been was empty. The salesman had been telling the truth and he had saved Cialdini the pain of regret. Cialdini spoke with his manager and commended him for the great job he was doing. The tactics of urgency and scarcity work when you are in integrity.

When you are guiding a client through the close, your attitude might feel pushy or used-car-sales-y if you are out of integrity. You must be in integrity. You want to cultivate an attitude of loving the person enough that you don't want them to experience a sense of regret. You don't want them to miss out on your service, and neither do they. You want them to get all they can out of this life experience.

Using the Premier Package

A few years ago Shannon and I went to the Dominican Republic to pick up our oldest daughter from a service mission. While visiting the country we decided to take a dune buggy tour of the local area. As we gathered with a group of about thirty other people before the tour began, a guide approached us and asked if we would be interested in their private VIP option. For $50 more per person, we could have a private guide on the tour. In addition, we would be able to go at our own pace, leaving any stop when we were ready instead of waiting for everyone else. To top it off, we would get to the final beach destination about forty-five minutes before the rest of the group.

What would you do? Would it be worth it for an extra $150 to you? In that moment as we were waiting with the large group, it was worth it for me and we signed up. Later, while relaxing alone on the beach, I felt it was $150 very well spent.

Have you ever paid to have an enhanced experience? Have you ever purchased an extra item so that you could get the free gift? I would bet that you have done so at one time or another. Your clients splurge too, and they are willing to pay extra to you if you make them the right offer.

If you'd like to have your clients requesting to give you more money than the cost of your services, then master using the premier package offer.

When you initially introduce a price point to a client, you often have very little idea of how restrictive their budget is. You can ask great questions and use their eye movements to get more information from them. You can also use the premier offer closing tool to help you gauge their cost-consciousness.

As I present my service to a client, I often begin with the standard package that is a great value and will meet all of their needs. If you are in the medical industry, you can use this when you are selling to someone who doesn't have insurance. While I am educating them about the standard service, I point out that the package is not the premier package, and then I continue the conversation.

Let's pretend for a moment that you and I are sitting across the table from one another. I have just finished the presentation for the thing you want and now I am going to share the investment with you.

"So, John, the total investment for the thing you came here for is only $1,000. That will give you everything you said you wanted and all the necessary product to make sure you have a great outcome. Now, it's not our Premier Package, but it will give you everything you asked for."

What is the very next question John is going to ask 99.99% of the time?

Of course the answer is, "What's the Premier Package?" (I swear I heard you say it out loud as I typed this.)

For most people, that simple statement of introducing a VIP package, backed up with the assurity that they are going to get what they came here for, is a trigger. The curiosity will be too great for them not to ask.

What do you add to your premier package? Whatever you think would make them say 'Yes.' This package allows you to showcase the amazing service you are capable of providing. Maybe it's premier appointment times, a reserved parking spot or some other white-glove service. Maybe it includes a warranty or other additional value. The point is to have layers of service and to give your clients the opportunity to choose the one that suits them best. A certain percentage of your current clients will pay extra for premier service.

You can create your premier package however you want. There are only a few rules:

1. Add in items that have a high perceived value but a low cost to you.

2. Only add in things you are 100% going to deliver.

3. Make sure the enhancements compliment the service the client originally came in for and will help them be successful in their desired outcome.

4. Do not set the premier price so low that everyone will say 'Yes.' This may seem like an obvious rule, but this happens more than you might think.

Other than that, you can create how you want and charge accordingly.

When I recently taught a coaching group about this new scaling opportunity, the treatment coordinator in an orthodontic office responded that offering a VIP package to their patients would be a really tough sell considering her client demographic. "No one wants to spend a penny more on treatment than they have to," she predicted.

I agreed that this could be true and then challenged her to try it out during the next week. I promised her that if I was wrong, I would never speak to her about the up-sell again and she would never have to think about it. She reluctantly dedicated herself to the seven-day challenge.

Seven days later, she almost couldn't contain her excitement as she told us about her experience.

"We put together a $450 VIP Package that consisted of a whitening kit, electric toothbrush, special parking spot in front of the building and an extra retainer at the end of treatment. I presented it just like you taught us, and I can't believe that people said, 'Yes.'"

Excited for her, I followed up with the question, "Was anyone who did not accept the offer offended or upset that you made the offer?"

"No. No one was," she exclaimed before stopping herself and saying, "Well, actually that is not true. No one said 'No' to the offer, so I don't know."

She had achieved a 100% closing ratio on the VIP offer. Some people even said 'Yes' to her after previously claiming to be shopping around before the VIP offer was made.

However you choose to use the premium offer, the point is to give more of what they want and to bring more money into your business. There is no limit on what you can offer and what you can charge as long as you are truly giving something of value.

VIRTUAL REALITY

What premier services could you offer to your clients?
How can you feature these white-glove amenities to them?

Introducing the Stack

A closing technique that is foundational in my business is the stack. If you are in a commodity market, the only way to set yourself apart is to build value, and the stack can help you do just that. For example, let's take a look at the cell phone market. I love my Samsung Note, especially the dark mode because I often get ideas when I'm in bed at night and I can just grab my stylus, make a few notes on my phone, and then go back to sleep. Though it's a great phone, there's really nothing unique about it. A dozen different phone companies are selling the same model. Cell companies use the stack to compete in a commodity industry. They sell the same models but offer better Wi-Fi or an incredible data plan to build the stack.

Anyone can go and get a Samsung Note at any of those stores for around $1,000. So how could I get someone to pay $5,000 for it?

Here's how. When I load the phone with all of the training I have created over the last decade of selling through the screen, I could sell it for $5,000. I would include techniques that I have personally used to sell over a million dollars with. I would employ recorded case studies with clients who have increased their business by 15, 20 or 30%. All of the sudden, that $1,000 phone is worth more than the commodity itself. Especially when, as a bonus, Ryan Gosling's personal cell phone number is also stored in the phone's contacts.

What you have to sell is the value of the product. Everything else you do is going to be pointing to that value, increasing the value of what you're giving, so when you reveal the bottom line. As an example, you could show a slide on a monitor that breaks down the stack to look something like this. If you don't have the ability to generate a slide, have a piece of paper to either have it pre-broken down or hand write the numbers. Just have it visual. People want to see what they are getting.

Awesome Graphic Design

Proposal for Jane Author's $1,000,000 Generating Book Cover

INCLUDED
- Unlimited Design Alterations $783.00
- 3D Cover for Social Media $1652.00
- Kindle and E-Reader files $1140.00
- Post- locked Adjustments for 6 mo. $1237.00
- Completed Design Files for Future $5557.00
- Personal Branding Guide $1589.00
- 6 Sessions of expanded brand coaching $2678.00

} Complimentary Value $14,457.00

Total Investment $6789

Remember, visual is memorable, so do what you can to not only tell them what the discounts are, show them. From calling it a "Million Dollar Smile", which sets a really high number in their head, to showing them that how much you are including is actually higher than their final amount, all of this helps them see how much they are gaining vs paying. When they see the numbers broken down between the value of what you are including, as well as any discounts, the number they are paying becomes more manageable.

Because so many people are asking, and because I want you to be successful, and because you've gotten a great sense of who I am and what I do in this book, and because you can see my value, would you be opposed to me sharing with you the new, irresistible program I have so you can continue your education on this journey?

I can teach you how to implement these practices in your office through a program called the **Selling Through the Screen**

Blueprint, and it's unlike anything you've seen before. This program will dive deeper into virtual sales to help your business succeed. I will show you how to make these principles more malleable so that they fit into your unique business model. This intensive training program includes:

- **4 weeks of self-guided coaching (value $4,497.00)**
  - The most important thing you need is NOT information. No one actually needs to purchase more information. What you need is more understanding on how to use the tools you have, the new tools you learned while reading and to be able to create new tools specifically designed for you and your practice. That is what the self-guided coaching allows you to do. You will follow along with me as I coach a group of practice owners, answer their questions and share in each others' successes.
- **5-day challenge archives (value $997.00)**
  - Would you like to share what you learned in this book with your team but realize the chances of all of them reading this book are slim to none? Instead have them follow along as I hold the live classes of the Selling Through the Screen Challenge. They can watch and learn through the video training portal.
- **PDF worksheets for your team - test and implement (value $97.00)**
  - Have your team follow along, take notes and create a personal reference binder with the PDFs included.

In this book I have tried to be thorough in my teaching without overwhelming the reader. However, many things, especially when we're talking body language, simply do not translate onto the page the same way as when you view them on the screen.

The **Selling Through the Screen Blueprint** package has a value of over $5,500, but because you read this far in the book and because I know you want to succeed as quickly as you can, I am offering it for $497.

However, I want to make sure you have everything you need to succeed as fast as possible. So, I have decided to throw in a few extras for you at no additional charge.

Many on your team will push against the idea of role playing or complain about not understanding how to do it correctly. So I have solved that challenge for you by creating a role play video library for you and your team to watch, follow along, quiz themselves and practice with. This is what I call my Role Play Video Vault.

- **Bonus #1: Role play video vault (value $3,497.00)**
  - This is the Netflix of body language training. With over 50 videos in the portal, you and your team see me and others tackle what we talk about in this book to see what to say and how to say it as well as how to close the deal.
  - We will go more in depth in body language training as we cover the Eyes, feet/legs, face, hands and more.

It's a fact, if you do not have the right players in the right seats, your life is going to be way more challenging. Having a proven and powerful way to find the superstars who want to work with you and have a system to love those who are not a fit for you into another job is crucial for your ultimate success. That is why I wrote the book and created the program Hire & Fire Like a Boss.

- **Bonus #2: Hire & Fire Like a Boss Digital Course (Value $997)**

The new total value of this program, including all of the bonuses, is over $10,000. You will receive all of that for $497.

Selling Through the Screen Blueprint

Total Value: Over $10,000.00
Today: $497.00

- **4 weeks of self-guided coaching (value $4,487.00)**
- **5-day challenge archives (value $997.00)**
- **PDF worksheets for your team - test and implement (value $97.00)**
- **Bonus #1: Role play video vault (value $3,480.00)**
- **Bonus #2: Hire & Fire Like a Boss Digital Course (Value $948)**

At this point, because you are an intelligent, discerning reader, you would ask me a certain question if we were together face-to-face. Whenever you find yourself negotiating a price, don't forget to use: "Is that the best you can do?"

It's an amazing question. I know that you have invested time, effort and energy into reading this book. Because of that, I'm going to reward you with a special price. When you go to https://www.sellingthroughthescreen.com/salesblueprint, you'll receive this entire value for $497. Each of my clients will have the opportunity to enroll in the Selling Through the Screen Blueprint, but not at this special price.

This is a program that can transform the way you approach the virtual examination process within your practice. You have the opportunity to enroll, but I also know that if you choose not to, you are doing it for one of three reasons. Either you don't trust me, you don't trust yourself, or you don't really care about Selling Through the Screen either way.

Creating your own stack

Did you feel compelled as I presented that stack? Even as you simply read through the words in this book, were you drawn in? You can create this same sense of your service's value in your own business. Go through your services and create a detailed list of everything that your business offers. If you are a pest control company, you initially perform an analysis of the property, including a consultation with the owner about any needs. You make quarterly visits to maintain the property. You have a 24-hour hotline for your clients in case of an emergency. You are insured and accredited. You offer a complementary lawn consultation. Whatever your business is, whatever your list looks like, get it lined out and really bring home the value of each of those services to your prospective client.

When you stack the value of all of those services, your clients will start working the numbers in their head and see that you are really offering a $2,000 annual service for just $97 per quarter. You will help them see what they are getting financially, and they will get excited about what they want and move forward.

That is the power of the stack.

I love selling and being sold to! I love the power of sales and the way it allows me to help people avoid the pain of regret. I love people enough to want to help them get what they want. I hope you learned so much from reading about my stacked offer. As you create your own sales stack, you will be able to see for yourself the massive, insane value that you are offering people. You want them to realize that they would be crazy not to work with you.

VIRTUAL REALITY

List 5-10 items you could include in your own stack. List the value of each product and then list what bonuses you want to include to make your offer irresistible.

_____

_____

_____

_____

_____

_____

The 5 Objections

At the beginning of this book we evaluated the three reasons people say 'No' to an offer: either they don't trust themselves, they don't trust you, or they don't really want to move forward. These three reasons go hand-in-hand with five objections that people will give you as an excuse not to move forward. People will often use objections as smoke screens when not wanting to make a commitment.

It is important to understand that there is a difference between an objection and a condition. An objection is a reason for disagreement. A condition is an event or situation that makes it unlikely, irresponsible, illegal or even immoral for the client to move forward. Yes, those are my own guidelines.

Some companies have policy conditions to help them navigate ethical situations. For example, home alarm companies have policies that do not allow them to sell to people who are renting their home or who know they will be moving in the next twelve months. If your potential client has recently lost their job, filed bankruptcy and will soon be living in their car, a policy condition might specify that it would be unwise for them to invest in your product.

I think you get the picture.

When it comes to objections, there are really only five categories of them, and we can take a closer look at each one to help you address or even preempt them from stalling the close.

Objection 1: Time.

- I didn't realize it would take that long
- I don't think the timing is right
- That sounds like it's going to take a lot of work

We are all limited by a certain number of hours and minutes in the day, and some people use their limited time as an excuse.

Objection 2: Money.

- That's more expensive than I planned
- I don't think that will work with my budget
- I might be able to get a better price somewhere else

This is the objection where return on investment is central.

Objection 3: Others.

- I'll have to talk to my spouse
- I'm not sure if I'll get buy-in from my team
- I need to run this by my parents

People will use this objection to deflect responsibility onto someone else. They want to confer with another person and get validation for their decision.

Objection 4: Fear.

- I'm not sure that this will work out
- I don't know if I can make that happen
- I don't know if I will get the results I want

Some people allow fear to keep them from taking the next step in their lives. They want surety or some guarantee that this product or service will work out for them. Whatever your industry, be sure to develop some kind of guarantee program to present whenever a fear-based objection comes up.

For instance, if you are in orthodontics you can offer a Smile Guarantee program. You can let prospective clients know that whether or not they wear the retainers, if in the future they need another treatment, you will take care of them for a small monthly fee. You can offer some sort of back-up plan to set the client's mind at ease, just be sure that the client also bears the risk.

Objection 5: Shame

- I'm embarrassed that I need help with this
- I can't believe I'm having this problem again
- I should be able to do this on my own

When shame is at the root of an objection, the client will rarely admit it outright. It may take some discerning questions to better understand where they are coming from.

ADDRESSING OBJECTIONS

As you craft a game plan for your virtual sales process, you will want to tailor your marketing message to address these five objections. You can build messaging to address time, money, others, fear and shame right into your marketing. If you notice one type of objection is occurring more often than others, adjust your marketing to address the objection ahead of time. Create a message to let people know that your service is different than they might expect.

If your small business were a restaurant, your marketing team would be the hosts and hostesses. They are out among the tables, talking with the patrons, getting a pulse of what is happening in the community and how best to serve. Your marketing team will communicate through billboards, postcards or other advertising to create buzz and draw people unto your restaurant. However, the salespeople are the ones actually putting in the orders. They're the ones who close. So it is imperative that your marketing team and your sales team have consistent communication to make sure your marketing message is matching your closing clientele. I would recommend a meeting between these two departments at least monthly.

When I work with a business owner to help raise their close rates, I investigate the objections their potential clients are making and look for patterns. We look at how the time of year, competitors' offers or other factors are affecting closing rates. After we have amassed some data we build marketing copy to address each objection. We revamp the scripting for the intake calls, landing pages and sales presentations with one goal in mind: enter the conversation in the client's head, identify the objections, and address them before they confess them.

Examples of how to address objections:

- If you're like most of our best clients, you might be asking what the investment is for this program, and we totally understand that.
- Many of our clients have wondered before they met us if we were a good fit for them.
- What we've heard before is that our clients are asking themselves if our service can meet their needs.

- What we've found is that people are wondering if this treatment will give them the results they are looking for.

- You're not alone if you are thinking of what your spouse will say about this program.

- It's very common for people to be curious about price, and we get that.

As you can see from these examples, you don't have to *answer* an objection to address it. Addressing the objection is simply a verbal acknowledgement that the concern exists. Answering the question is not as important to people as bringing it up before they do. When a client hears you acknowledge their question it allows them psychologically to move past the unknown.

As you create this marketing copy, you want to come up with language that is so authentic to you that it sounds just like your natural conversation. You are going to practice it so much that it flows right out of your mouth and no one would ever imagine that you were reading from a script. Years ago I heard the expression, "The only thing that will mess this up is your better idea." I love the way this phrase helps other people open up to a new perspective, so I use it all the time. It's part of my verbiage now, a Dino-ism, so much so that I don't even remember where I first heard it. We want a sales script or sales template with that sort of dynamism and authenticity.

I love the imagery Amy Demas has developed while teaching front desk people how to make a great impression. In her insightful book *Communicate Excellence*, Amy describes each exchange of information with a client as filling a bucket. Your team would have certain buckets that they need to fill, in no particular order, before advancing a client to the next step. This process allows you to inform, vet, and prepare your potential clients before you see them at the virtual presentation.

Another way to preempt objections is to build scripting that will help prepare your clients for a successful virtual presentation. This works especially well with the spouse objection.

A simple question your phone ninjas can use to address the I-need-to-talk-to-my-spouse objection:

Josie: Will all of the deciding parties be on the call when we do our virtual appointment?

Spencer: No, but I can relay the information to my wife afterwards.

Josie: When we meet with you, we are prepared to get things going for you that same day. Because it's a virtual consultation, we're super flexible with our times so we can have both of you at the appointment. Another great option is having them Skype or Facetime in during the call. How can we get both of you there during the appointment?

Do you see how Josie clears this hurdle before the sales presentation even begins? This is how you want to structure your process, overcoming objections before they even become an issue.

Clarify the conversation

As you are wrapping up the intake process, whether using an electronic intake form or over the phone, you can use these questions to prime the prospect. Try asking your version of the following to get more information and to stimulate people's thinking.

Josie: What is the best result you could get from our program?

Spencer: My son could feel more confident in his smile. It would be great to see him not hide his mouth with his hands so much.

Josie: Awesome, thanks for sharing that. Confidence is such a big deal for young people, and watching your kids struggle is never easy.

Spencer: Yeah.

Josie:	Yeah. And what about the worst result you could get from our program?
Spencer:	He might still have some problems. He may never have the smile he wants.
Josie:	Yeah, I understand that. It's difficult to gauge how each individual is going to respond to treatment. It might set your mind at ease to know that 93% of our clients would recommend us to others, so we do have a great success rate.
Spencer:	Nice. That's good to know.
Josie:	Yeah. So Spencer, on a scale of 1-10, 1 being you are not really interested in the program right now, you are just shopping around, and 10 being you are ready to start, you are just trying to find the right program, where are you on that scale?
Spencer:	I'd say I'm a 7 right now.
Josie:	That's great. So you're getting serious, you're ready to do something to get different results. I have just one more question for you. What would it take for us to make sure that your experience is so amazing that it becomes a 10 by the time we get to the end of the presentation?

Do you see how Josie is able to clarify the conversation and get a solid understanding of where her prospect is through these final questions? Asking what the best and worst result is will help people imagine what is possible with your service. When you are asking the scale of 1-10 question, if the person is ranking themself lower than a 4, just thank them and end the call. But if they are more serious about your service, go ahead and ask them what is really important to them.

Companies often miss an opportunity to clarify the client's desires on the first phone call. We often go into data mode and take down the particulars, and the client is usually in data mode as well. Instead, you need to gather information while priming people to say 'Yes' to you. You need to help them to see themselves with the amazing results you offer. Go ahead and ask what could make their experience so amazing that it would be a no-brainer for them.

Your marketing message should help to alleviate client objections by design. If you hear the same objections more than a few times in a week, change your messaging. You can preempt concerns about time, money, others, fear and shame through your marketing and filtering process.

Client Surveys

At the 8th grade dance, I had no idea what Angela Sandaval was looking for. Our communication involved ... guesswork. In order to excel at what you do and maintain an excellent customer experience, it is crucial that you know what your clients want. Sometimes we make assumptions about what people are looking for because we're not really asking. To take the guesswork out of business, I love to send out surveys to my clients to discover that they are looking for.

Some business owners act like Steve Jobs. Instead of asking people what they want, he creates something and then tells people that they want it. Henry Ford is quoted as saying, "If I had asked people what they wanted, they would have said, 'Faster horses.'" If you are a technology maven or are literally trying to reinvent the wheel, these tactics might be valuable. However, there is also great value in understanding what people want so you can deliver within the context of what you can do.

Surveys are important. They can show you what people want, from your clients to your team members. Ask, don't assume, so you can get insights to help guide your business. Asking is no guarantee that you will implement every idea, but it will give you data so you can look for patterns and adjust your approach.

Advantages of Surveying

- Uncover the answers and find the gaps
- Evoke discussion
- Become objective in your decision making
- Make progress
- Find out how your team members are doing

Uncover the answers and find the gaps

The greatest business minds are those who have learned to see things from a different perspective. I often see business owners who have gotten used to their own view of how their business is performing and are missing out on understanding how things look from their clients' or their team's perspective. Surveys will help you identify the gap between your perception of the marketplace and the realities of the marketplace.

A great way to begin tapping into your clients' or team's insights is to do an exercise called the Fives. Send out a survey that asks them to list five things the business is amazing at and five things the business can improve upon. This can be an invaluable tool in understanding what it really feels like to be your client or your team member. If you have eight people on your team and each of them lists their top five, you'll suddenly have forty different areas to look at and improve upon. You'll be able to see which areas crossover between several people so you can work on those more crucial areas first.

Evoke discussion

The goal of gathering data from the people around you is to expand your perspective and create further discussion. Our businesses can be living, breathing things that change to better serve and support our teams and our clients. Just because you've always done something one way does not make it the best way, and we're going for the best.

Surveys can be an important part of your business culture because of what happens with your team when you allow everyone to have a voice. When you ask where everyone wants to go for a company retreat, you get buy-in! People will be excited about the direction you are heading. I try to implement as many ideas from my team as possible, because people support what they help create. The more you can get your team to create with you, the more enrolled they will become in your programs and your business. And the quickest way to get creative data from your entire team is through a survey. Don't be afraid to ask for their ideas or opinions. Set up the premise that not every idea will be implemented and that implementation will take time, then invite your team's perspective.

Whenever I do a 2-day office evaluation for a client I send out a survey to every member of their team before I come in. I ask 10 questions so when I am with the team in the office for those two days I come prepared. This data is not biased by the perception of the business owner, it's raw data. As I consult with the owner I often find that they have one idea of how their office culture is going, and their team has an entirely different view. The data opens the way for discussing new solutions and strategies with the owner. When you survey your team, it's best to do a blind survey. You don't want your team to be concerned about repercussions, you want them to feel free to give unfiltered feedback.

VIRTUAL REALITY

When it comes to your team members, what one survey question would you like to know the answer to most?

Become objective in your decision making

When human beings are faced with a problem, the higher their emotion is, the lower their IQ. Emotion can cause confusion in our bodies and shut down our thinking processes. We can become so caught up in the discomfort of the emotion that we are no longer able to think clearly.

Raw data from a blind survey can help us all overcome this emotion. And I get it, businesses are emotional. We spend so much time and energy in our businesses, we risk for our businesses, we put our hearts into our businesses. You may fear that during the survey process people will tell you something you don't want to know. Even if you are growth-minded, feedback can carry a little bit of sting to it. However, feedback will also help us make better decisions.

When you review your survey data, try to approach the feedback with a sense of curiosity and non-attachment. Let go of judgment and embrace the new data to help you move forward.

Make progress and stay relevant

Surveys will allow you to be creative as you navigate in your industry. As you come up with new ideas you can try them out on your clients beforehand through a survey. You'll be making decisions based on what your clients think, not what you think they think.

Mentimeter is a survey tool that I love to use in consultations and presentations. This tool allows you to survey your team or audience on their devices, and their answers populate a fun word cloud that you can display. Mentimeter is an anonymous group-think exercise that allows the entire audience to participate and learn together. Survey Monkey is another great option for survey creation. The Facebook Survey tool can also come in handy for basic surveys.

In recent surveys I conducted, I've discovered that many salespeople are concerned that their clients will not respond as well to their programs if they offer them virtually. They think selling through the screen might somehow cheapen the service. But they are guessing. If you are feeling this concern, have you asked? Have you surveyed your clients? You can't know until you ask.

Find out how your team members are doing

If you have ever called into Delta Airlines you will be asked to participate in a brief, one question survey after your call. What does the question say? (I am paraphrasing) "On a scale of 1-5, if you had to hire the representative you spoke with, how likely would you do so."

What a great question to find out how people think of the service they received by that specific person. Also, if your team members knew they were being scored on a question like that, do you think they might be more alert, aware and focused on being the best representative for your company as they could be? I do.

Challenge #7: Create a survey.

For this challenge, you are going to create a survey for your clients. You'll want to ask a minimum of four questions. The intent is for you to explore what your clients want their experience to look like, what they are concerned about, and what you can do to make the experience better.

You may choose to create an exit survey to give to your clients after you have wrapped up the service. Exit surveys are so helpful in business because of the data they provide about value and how you can improve. A good exit survey has about 5-8 questions that a client can answer very quickly.

There is a simple science to creating a great survey. The questions that will give you the most data will be ranking questions, the ones your clients are going to answer on a scale of 1-5. The next best questions are multiple choice. Reserve any fill-in-the-blank questions for the very end. Survey Monkey, a Google form or a Facebook survey are all great platforms you can use.

For an added bonus, create a video of yourself asking the survey questions to your clients. Practice genuine curiosity and willingness to meet your clients' needs during the video. And don't forget to strike your power pose beforehand!

Expert Interview: Real World Virtual Exams with Startaloo's Dr. Anthony Bonavoglia

It was 2007. The United States was on the cusp of a major real estate market collapse that would cause financial havoc worldwide, and Dr. Anthony Bonavoglia was running out of options. His wife was six months pregnant. His contract as an associate was about to expire, and his opportunities to buy into a partnership had fallen apart one by one. As a last-ditch effort he decided to go through the phone book and call each orthodontic office in Hudson Valley, New York where he and his wife wanted to live. Many of these phone calls were dead ends, but one orthodontist told Bonavoglia to come up and see him.

It was a seven hour drive but Bonavoglia had a good feeling about it, so he made the trip and met with the orthodontist. He learned that there was no practice to buy, there was only a building. The orthodontist asked Bonavoglia to propose something and he went for it. Out of these unconventional beginnings, Bonavoglia's practice was born.

He decided not to get a loan for his start-up. He used what he had in the bank to start the practice, so in the beginning Bonavoglia was the sole team member in his practice. He did everything from scheduling patients to cleaning chairs, assisting himself like when he was back in dental school. Instead of a practice management system, he used a book and an Excel spreadsheet. Building a practice from the ground up taught him how to grind. It gave him a unique perspective and the ability to see the inefficiencies in the system. He began borrowing solutions from other industries and was excited to bring them into his practice. This start-up would eventually grow to a team of 25 that starts 800 patients each year. Bonavoglia recently decided to commercialize his orthodontic solutions and launched Startaloo.

Startaloo is a pending patient solution that can help practices navigate the world of virtual sales. It's tools include 1) a fully-automated presentation, 2) robust data analysis and 3) follow-up support for pending clients. Bonavoglia wanted to hire a TC with personality first, so he built a customizable presentation that crunches the numbers automatically. He knew there was money to be made in usable data, so he worked with data analysts to capture that information. He didn't want to let clients slip through the cracks, so he designed a follow-up system that uses psychology to guide the client to the close. "If you've ever seen the movie Moneyball, you might have an idea of what we are doing," Bonavoglia explained.

He built his service as an off-site company that uses virtual assistants to support practices. Each presentation and follow-up is fully customizable, so the patient has no idea the support is coming from a remote office. Startaloo has been very effective for a lot of practices, and 100% of their patients are followed up with appropriately.

"If I go on a date with someone for the first time and then wait two weeks to call them back, I'm not getting a second date," Bonavoglia illustrates. His follow-up process uses sales data to determine exactly when to send a text, an email, or pick up the phone.

But what really gets Bonavoglia excited is data analysis. He has learned how to strip out the noise in the numbers and focus on things he can change to bring more clients into his practice. He has built tools that show which TCs resonate better with adolescents than adults and who needs training in liners. He can show you actual conversion rates, lag times, and production values. By using heat maps and splitting out the data by demographic, he can tell you where to invest your marketing dollars to make the biggest impact.

"Every time you do a presentation, you are losing data," Bonavoglia asserts. " If you're not capturing the information — not just on who you start, but who you don't start — you've lost the opportunity to grow." To learn more about Startaloo and how it's tools can support your practice, visit Startaloo.com.

8

Advanced Sales Skills

For those of you who are ready to go beyond the basics and really get into the process of implementing virtual sales strategies in your business, this chapter is for you. If you are ready for next-level sales, buckle up for these advanced strategies.

Teach, Tailor, Take Control

One high-level goal that many entrepreneurs are reaching for is a legacy following. This type of client loyalty means that rather than having to market repeatedly to your clientele every time they need your service, they simply come back to you. You no longer have to prove your worth every time because the decision to go with your company is already firmly in their minds. These clients are thinking long-term. The question is, how do you create a business model that is going to result in a legacy clientele?

In the book *The Challenger Sale*, the authors point to a 2011 study from the Consumer Research Group. The CRG conducted a study to try to answer this question about legacy clientele. The first thing they did was define what it means to be a loyal consumer. The CRG criteria for a loyal clientele are:

1. Clients who are advocates for your brand and they will tell others without being prompted
2. Clients who are excited to buy from you right now
3. Clients who are willing to buy more in the future and bring their family without price shopping for new offers

The result of this study of 5,000 consumers was astounding. It turns a lot of conventional wisdom on its head. You may be thinking that price-point is a major driver of client loyalty, but only 9% of the consumers chose price as a loyalty driver. Even company performance, or how the company actually performed compared to its competitors, only accounted for 38% of client loyalty. A full 53% of consumers indicated that the one reason they were loyal to a brand was because of the sales experience.

To create a legacy program, your sales experience must be top-notch. From the very first contact to the close, what matters most is not price. It's not even how well you perform your service. It's the experience people have during the sales process. In order to help you instill this magnetic brand loyalty, let's explore three ways you can give your clients a sales experience unlike anything else.

TEACH

Now more than ever, people are looking for guidance. The flow of the world has shifted so much that they are seeking information they can use to restructure their lives. They are looking for businesses that teach what's in it for them. They want to be shown why they should care about what you have to offer. People aren't interested in what school you went to or what awards your business has won. They want to know what kind of a difference your service will make in their lives and why it is relevant to them.

When I market for my Selling Through the Screen programs, I tell people exactly why they need to learn how to sell virtually. I show them how much the marketplace is changing, and how essential it is to be nimble and forward-thinking. I show them that they are not going to find another program anywhere that will walk them through this transition like the program I offer.

One great truism in the marketing world is to **enter the conversation that is already happening inside your client's head**. What are they thinking? What is their biggest worry? What do they want?

You can answer these questions the old-fashioned way, which is by guessing. Or you can use a survey and discover exactly what the client wants. When you uncover this data from your client base, you will know what they are looking for and exactly what you need to teach.

Craft marketing pieces that inform. Teach people what you have discovered in your industry. People will be drawn to your content as it presents relevant information that will affect their lives. If you are a carpet cleaning company, don't lead your marketing with how you are better than the competition. Instead educate people on the *5 Dangers that are Creeping Around in Your Carpet Right Now*. Create a piece called *7 Mistakes People Make When It Comes to* X, or *3 Ways Why* Y *Might Not Be Right for You*. These are the questions your clients are already asking, and when your business is the one answering them, people are going to respond.

TAILOR

You may be tempted to make sure that every human being within your reach can hear your marketing message. You may think that casting a wide net will result in a thriving business. However, experience across many industries shows that when you tailor your message to meet the needs of your ideal client, a loyal clientele follows. A tailored marketing focus creates an exclusive clientele of people who want to do business with you and are willing to pay a higher price for that privilege.

A few years ago I read a news story about a female dentist who was just opening up a new practice and had already booked out appointments for the first two months. For most new businesses, booking clientele takes months to establish. Everyone wanted to know how she did it. It turned out that every Friday night during construction this savvy dentist hosted a wine and cheese night for ladies in her area. At the ribbon-cutting for her practice she revealed the interior design and it looked more like a spa than a dental office. This entrepreneur knew who her ideal client was. She tailored every aspect of her business model to draw them to her and won.

If you have been using the wide-net marketing theory in your business, it's time to focus in and figure out who you really want to be working with. What age group? What demographic? What specific need are you looking to fill? Take a look at which clients you are most excited to take on and start there.

TAKE CONTROL

As an entrepreneur, a professional, or a salesperson, you must learn how to take control of your own business. You assume the sale every time, knowing that the client sought you out. You are in control of which services you are willing to let them invest in.

As I was conducting the live Selling Through the Screen Challenge, I gave people the opportunity to participate in an advanced group coaching program. A couple of people emailed me because they were interested in individual coaching sessions, which was different from what I was offering. I had already made my business plan and I was doing group coaching, not individual sessions. So I once again invited them to join the group program that I had created and allowed them to choose in or not.

I had someone else reach out to me who wanted to get into a program after the deadline and wanted to pay the discounted price. This person had a lot of excuses for why I should bend the rules for him. I reiterated my terms to him and when he continued to argue, I used 'Nevertheless' to bring the conversation to a close. Now, I always try not to be attached to the outcome with a possible client, but after this conversation I was a little worked up. In my mind I was thinking, "How dare you ask me to break my own integrity?"

If you are in sales, you are in control of bringing the money in for your business. Your job is to grow the business. If you are behaving in a way that is passive and beta, it's time to step up to the plate. You are the person offering this service. You get to set the parameters and take control.

I'm a pretty nice guy. I'm not exactly the domineering male in a white tank top. But when it comes to my business, I am a benevolent alpha. I want you to learn how to stand firm in the boundaries that you set for yourself and for your company. When you have a client who is pushing those parameters, I want you to take the internal stance of 'How dare you ask me to break my integrity and the integrity of this company?' Allow them to choose in or choose out. If they go with someone else, the only thing they won't be getting is you.

The Importance of Follow-Up: Mining the Diamonds

The minute a prospect walks out of your office or hits the exit button in the video call, the likelihood of that client closing with you decreases by 20%. Same-day starts are that important and we need to capture more of them, whether it's in-person or on-screen. However, unless a client gives you a 'Yes' or 'No' answer during the close, the sales process does not end with the presentation. You must have a killer follow-up protocol. This is not a suggestion, not a good idea, not 'we talked about it that one time and I can't remember who is on it but we'll reassign it when we think about it again.' I'm talking about an official procedure or system of rules governing how you help your clients avoid the pain of regret.

As a business owner or team member, it is your responsibility to follow-up to help your clients make a decision. I feel even more invested in enrolling people after they have seen me and not signed up yet, because the likelihood of them experiencing the pain of regret goes up each day they have not said 'Yes' to me. All I want, from every single person, is either a 'Yes' or a 'No,' and until I get a response, I'm going to continue educating and pursuing.

Setting up systems to take care of prospective clients after the sales presentation is more challenging than during any other phase. Many businesspeople have good follow-up *ideas* but very few actually implement those ideas, and they are missing out on opportunity. After the presentation, the heavy lifting is done. Having a robust follow-up protocol in place will give more clients the chance to say 'Yes' to you.

Remember that small actions can make a massive difference as you create your follow-up protocol. A candy store conducted an experiment to see how extra customer care would affect their candy sales. They ran the experiment for one week, dividing their visitors for that week into two groups. With the first group, the store manager met each visitor personally, greeted them warmly, and escorted them to the candy counter. With the second group, the store manager met each visitor personally, greeted them warmly, *gave them a piece of chocolate*, and then escorted them to the candy counter. Those visitors who were given candy purchased 42% more than those who did not get the candy. If you want your acceptance rate to skyrocket, the way you greet your clients and escort them through the process, whether you do it virtually or in-person, has to be a little bit different. Give people a little something that makes them want to give something back to you in return. In this case, a 'Yes' answer and their credit card information.

Great follow-up giveaways will follow Robert Cialdini's three rules: they are unexpected, personalized, and meaningful. You want to send something they did not need, want, or care about beforehand. If you do something for everyone all the time, it loses the element of surprise and becomes expected. Expected is not going to work the same magic. When a gift is personalized to a person's identity, their needs or their challenges, it shows that you took the time to consider them specifically. And now that the presentation is over and you have spent some time with the client, making your gift meaningful becomes a whole lot simpler.

During your interaction with the client, be on the lookout for those personal things they share with you to help you during the follow-up. You may decide to include an 'About Me' section on the intake form with a couple of questions to take out the guesswork. And by the way, if you are asking the client to share some of their favorites, don't forget to include some of your team's favorite things as well to help create that connection. Your clients will be much more likely to fill these questions out if you show them how to do it. When people know that your Director of First Impressions' favorite snack is chips and salsa, everyone becomes more humanized and more connected.

You and your team can become great investigators to get to know your clients better. If you work with kids, go ahead and focus on them. Even though the parents are ultimately making the decisions around purchasing, the focus on their child will trigger the parent.

The follow-up does not have to be expensive, just unique and different. I challenge you to create a follow-up protocol with a documented system of what will happen, when, and who is going to be in charge of each step. Just like everything else in your business, accountability is going to be essential to making the follow-up process stick.

Here's an example of what the process could look like:

- Within eight hours of a person leaving your office or signing off of the video call, they will receive a BombBomb great-to-meet-you video from you by email
- Twenty-four hours later, they will receive a follow-up phone call informing them of the next two available appointment times

- On day three they will receive a thank-you card in the mail
- On day four they will receive an email reiterating the financial breakdown with a link to sign up
- On day five they will receive a text invitation for them to ask you any questions

After these initial daily reach-outs you may decide to send a message less frequently, but I would recommend not letting more than three weeks go by without a reach-out.

When someone asks me how many times I want them to follow up with a client, my answer is always, "One more time." Keep chasing that 'Yes' or 'No' answer.

MAYBE

Alright, let's talk about 'Maybe.' There is nothing that frustrates a salesperson more than a 'Maybe' answer. It is Outer Darkness. It is the Sahara Desert. My advice is to aggressively pursue anyone who has not yet committed to a 'Yes' or 'No' answer. You may want to give up. You may think that one email sent or one unanswered phone call is enough. However, it is arrogance to believe that people are thinking of you as much as you are thinking of them. They have their own lives and they will completely forget you, happily. When you create a protocol to get a 'Yes' or 'No,' and understand that either one is acceptable, it will get you out of 'Maybe' purgatory.

The next time you are in the office, take a minute and write down the names of every client who has been relegated to your 'Maybe' list. Then send each one a text asking this question: **Have you completely given up on starting your service with us?** Asking this 'No' question will allow them to re-evaluate and give you a straight answer. As you employ this quick method, you will likely get responses from 50-70% of the people who were on the fence.

However you decide to follow up, be sure to have a solid system in place to do it. If you have an amazing service to offer, you can't drop a potential client the second time they don't pick up the phone. A follow-up system will check in with people until they commit. Otherwise, the answer is still 'Maybe,' and a 'Maybe' is something you keep pursuing.

VIRTUAL REALITY

What is your current follow-up practice? List three specific things you could do today to tighten up the follow-up process and bring in more clients.

_____

_____

_____

The 6 Gates to 'YES'

David Hoffeld is a sales guru who decided to investigate sales psychology scientifically. He researched the findings of over four hundred different studies on the human brain to discover how people make buying decisions. He concluded that there are six main areas that we need to be convinced in before we make a purchase. In order to get someone in your target market to say 'Yes' to you, there are six gates that you must guide them through. Any time you make any purchase, whether it's a major purchase like a new car or a minor purchase like breakfast cereal, you are going through these gates.

When it comes to training and tactics for salespeople, most are taught sales strategies instead of buying strategies. Most use sales tactics instead of buying tactics. Let's shift our perspective to buying mode so we can really get into our consumer's mind and figure out that it is they need. Let's enter the conversation already happening in their heads. Let's figure out what is keeping them up at night so we can provide the solution.

As you teach your prospects about your service, part of that instruction must address these six areas, or you will have a road-block. If you do successfully answer each area, people will move forward with you.

Gate 1: WHY CHANGE?

Why should I change? Why should I change who I am, what I look like, who I'm with, where I live, what car I drive, where I go, what I eat, what I wear?

One of the first things you learn in middle school science is Newton's first law of motion: An object at rest stays at rest unless acted on by an unbalanced force. This law of physics applies to humans, too. People naturally want to act the same way they acted yesterday unless they are given a good reason to change. Our brains are wired to associate change with risk. Our minds see novelty, from a new idea to a new product or service, as risky. As a person in sales or marketing, you are a risk factor. They have not yet developed trust with you, or they could have a bad experience with you. It's up to you to give them a reason to change, or they won't.

The good news is that just as people are wired to look at change as risky, we are also wired to have a desire for more. Whether you want more health, more energy, more money, or more hair, everyone has a universal desire for more. You can help clients want to change because they can get, be, do, or have more.

Gate 2: WHY NOW?

Why should I purchase now? What about this day, week, month, season, or year compels me to make this purchase?

In his studies on purchasing, Hoffeld discovered something most of us already know: the human brain naturally procrastinates. Being proactive is the exception, not the rule. Most people put off buying decisions, so we need to become more adept at helping people get to that buying mental space.

We want to help people avoid the pain of regret and commit to change happening now. Of course, you don't want to be an overbearing jerk. The pushy hustler routine simply does not work. However, you do want to help them realize that embracing change now rather than later is in their best interest.

You can use timing to help convince people to purchase from you. Figure out why now is the right time for your clients to make this change. It could be the best season or their phase of life. Every business is also tied by time. The fact is that you have a limited number of resources, appointments, and office space. You can use this built-in scarcity to create a marketing message around why now is the best time for your clients to choose into your business.

Gate 3: WHY YOUR INDUSTRY'S SOLUTION?

Why should I choose your solution? Why is this the best option out there for me?

This gate takes into account the many different options that people have in our high-tech and inter-connected world. Someone who wants to get their teeth straightened can choose the traditional doctor-led approach, or they can also turn to a mail-order service or teeth capping to improve their smile. Someone who is looking for their first place can rent a condo, build a starter home or buy a tiny house to live in. It's time to discover and then share the reasons why the solution your business offers is the best one for your clients.

Bold, direct advertising will help guide people to your specific solution. Teach people why your service is that thing they need. Don't be afraid to compare your solution to the other solutions out there. Trust that you know more than your prospective clientele does about what is going to be an amazing experience for them.

Gate 4: WHY YOU AND YOUR COMPANY?

Why should I choose your business? What makes you different from the others?

To guide prospects through this gateway, you are going to have to focus on you. This is where you zoom in and put your finger on what it is that makes your business culture unique. To stand out in your industry you can focus on one of two things: cost or differentiation. You can try to model your business after Walmart and be the low-cost leader, but there is zero competitive advantage to being the second low-price leader. Instead, be the premier provider and focus on what makes you stand out.

You will want to use social proof on multiple platforms, from shout-outs to case studies. I want you to use these pieces relentlessly and cycle them through repeatedly. Don't imagine that everyone has already seen your social proof. Another great way to present what sets your business apart is to write great content. Help educate people through a well-written news article or a relevant essay. There are local platforms in your area that are looking for good content, and you can supply it. Write that book. You may think that someone has already written the authoritative book in your industry, but it was not you. Your voice tells a different story and can change lives.

Reach out to top influencers and businesses in your area to develop a relationship with. Attorneys, contractors, accountants, sports teams, and dance schools can provide a link between you and your clients. Become a connector in your area by showing up in your local community. When you focus on your culture, people will be drawn to you.

VIRTUAL REALITY

What is uniquely attractive about your practice? How can you better feature this strength to your potential clientele?

Gate 5: WHY YOUR PRODUCT OR SERVICE?

Why is this product the best for me? Why will this service give me the results I need?

To get people through this gate, you get to bring a little brag into your education. Here's where you inform people why your product is the very best. You get to share the incredible features of your service and what makes it valuable to them. Focus on your warranty, your technology and other unique selling points.

For those of you who are thinking that your product isn't that different or stellar, consider a study that was conducted with the song "Twinkle, Twinkle, Little Star." In the United States, this tune tops the list of most popular nursery rhymes of all time. The study involved a person who tapped the beat of "Twinkle, Twinkle, Little Star" on a desk with a pencil. A group of twenty people were asked to listen to the beat and try to name the song. Not a single person could guess the song, though every one of them was very familiar with it. The tapped beat alone was not enough to bring the tune to mind.

This study is a great example of the *curse of knowledge*, a phenomenon that occurs when a person who is communicating with other people assumes that everyone has the background to understand their information. This knowledge bias is the bane of expertise, when something is so familiar to you that you forget that others could find it new or fascinating.

When you are educating your prospects about your product or service, don't let knowledge bias get in your way. Don't assume that everyone already knows about what you are offering. Break it down and make it simple to help them understand. Even if your competitor has it, explain it anyway. Act like nobody knows and tell them.

Gate 6: WHY SPEND THE MONEY?

Why should I give you my money? What about this opportunity compels me to part with my cash?

When you are asking someone to purchase something from you, you are also asking them not to purchase something else. I see a lot of businesses making huge mistakes when it comes to guiding people through this gate, and those mistakes are costing you money.

I love to watch Marcus Lemonis in the reality show "The Profit." Lemonis helps struggling small businesses by exchanging his expertise for a share of ownership in the business, but with one catch: the small business has to do everything Lemonis tells them to do. He can change their product line, paint their office or change their organizational structure. I would love to be like Marcus Lemonis and walk into a business and be 100% in charge. I see offices with old photos on the wall from the 70's and cringe, knowing what this is portraying to their clientele about how often they update their services. I see offices with huge TVs mounted in their waiting rooms and instead of showing marketing pieces featuring their businesses, they are featuring content with commercials for other businesses. I see coffee tables piled with magazines containing spread after spread of advertising. If you want people to spend their money with you, stop advertising other people's stuff in your offices.

Everything in or around your business, from your website to your building, should be branded to you. When you walk through Disneyland, you don't see any other brands in the theme park. Everything in that space is branded to Disney. Even the Dasani water or the Coke is paired with Disney branding. When you have a prospective client in your space, you want them to be thinking about you and your product. When you have someone else's advertisements in your space, they are taking money out of your pocket. The next time you walk through your office, keep branding in mind. Your business may be past due for a makeover ditching other people's advertising and redirecting attention back to you.

Your marketing must appeal to people's dominating buying motives, or their emotional reasons for buying. There are two scientifically documented triggers of human behavior around why people purchase things: a desire for gain and a fear of loss. Though neuroscience proves that fear of loss is a much bigger motivator, don't evoke fear unless you reveal how the buyer can escape fear through your service's benefits. Though you don't want to scare people into buying from you, you do have a moral obligation to help them avoid the pain of regret.

In your next team meeting, I challenge you to discuss these six questions with your team. Go deep and get really clear on how to answer them for your clients. The next step is to audit all of your messaging, website, social media, scripts or templates and make sure they are answering each question. You can even send a survey to your existing clients to discover why they decided to change, why then, why they chose your industry's solution, why your business, why your product, and why they spent the money. Finding out what your clients really want will allow you to create engaging messaging. If you find your messaging is unclear, readjust. Guiding clients well through these Six Gates means you won't have to sell to people, they will sell to themselves.

Your #1 Job as a Business Owner

This one's for you, business owners! We're going to take a look at benevolent alpha leadership and the sales process to see if there are adjustments you can make to your process. I hope you understand that this is not a critique or a shame session, but an awareness session, an opportunity to learn and change. A great leader is always a learner who refuses to stop growing so they will continue to lead more effectively. In my experience with coaching sales teams, I have found that sometimes the biggest hindrance to the close is the owner. I've seen owners who don't know how to sell walk into a presentation and derail the sale. Often, your role is to simply not screw up the sale, and I'm going to show you how to do that.

But first, let's take a look at what priorities should drive you as a top-tier business owner:

Your #1 job is to grow your business. As the owner of your organization, you will become a leader for the people you invite into your business, whether they are team members or clients. Your highest priority is to be successful for those people. If you don't want that responsibility, you might consider going to work for someone else. Make no mistake that the responsibility of a business owner is a massive undertaking, and the following principles will help you rise to the challenge. When packaged together, these priorities will help you become a true leader and take care of everything in your business, including the people.

Your #1 promise is to run your organization as a business, not a hobby. You are going to run it like an owner rather than an operator. Showing up as a leader in your business means the buck stops with you.

VIRTUAL REALITY

Do you tend to operate your practice as a business or as a hobby? If you find yourself unable to make tough decisions for the health of your business, ask yourself why. Then listen.

Your #1 stance is to be the benevolent alpha so that everyone can win. To be clear, your job is not to be the nice guy or girl. You are not in your position to make everyone happy. Benevolent alphas know what they want. Their desires are so firm that they are not willing to let other people or other peoples' wants impede them. Even if people don't like the way you are leading, you must maintain a leader stance. You can create a leadership style that allows others to want to follow you, so you can get what you want without being a total jerk. A poor leader lacks vision, doesn't know what they truly believe, doesn't have goals, and is so worried about what other people will think about them that they don't focus on the business. You are going to overcome all of that and build a great leadership style to lead your business to success.

As an owner who prioritizes the success of the business over everything else, you won't care about your team members more than you care about the success of the business. That might seem heartless or callous, but you cannot bend to the desires of your team members to the detriment of your business. I was just working with an owner who was struggling with having to let a member of his team go. This team member had been with him for twenty-seven years and was really well-known in the community, but they were unwilling to change. As an owner, you have to let those people go. It is your vision that drives the business, and you'll need to let go of anyone who gets in the way of that vision.

When it comes to the sell, there are some things business owners do that will throw off the close. As we focus on these sales killers, determine which ones are holding you back in your business and make a plan to step it up.

SALES KILLERS

1. Messy environment

There is nothing that will turn off a prospective client like a cluttered office or backdrop. As my time working for Disney taught me years ago, *environment creates perception.* It is the owner's responsibility to keep things clean and professional-looking, whether you meet your clients in person or on the screen. As the one-ply toilet paper principle teaches us: You cannot promote yourself as a quality business while stocking your restrooms with one-ply toilet paper. Those thin squares communicate stinginess to your clients, and this perception will speak louder than your words. The overflowing trash can communicates neglectfulness to your clients. As you develop an online selling program, don't simply trust your team to have a clean, professional environment. Use the green screen and set up standards of environmental professionalism for your virtual consults.

2. Suggesting instead of Diagnosing

As a business owner, you must behave like one. You are the authority in your own business, and that confidence should radiate in your tone of voice and choice of words. A lot of people use sarcasm in their conversations, and though this form of communication can add humor and fun, don't use it during the first interaction with your clients. Sarcasm during the introductory meeting might indicate to the client that they can't trust you because they won't know what is serious and what's not. Instead, be friendly, jovial, and positive. After you have built a relationship, you can go ahead and use sarcasm to enhance that relationship. Until then, you are a professional, with knowledge and experience that your client is looking for. Diagnose with confidence.

3. Showing ambivalence

You must show up with an attitude of active concern and not ambivalence. Remove from your interactions phrases like, "Yeah, whatever, if you feel like it, we can probably help you." People are going to pay you for your certainty, so act the part. In the acting world, actors are encouraged to come to auditions in costume to help them get into character. Using a uniform, whether it's a company polo or professional attire, will help combat ambivalence. Uniforms create a psychological perception of authority, as illustrated nicely by the army and police forces. If you are in the medical profession and want to boost your sales rates, have your sales team wear white lab coats. From the time we are very young, we learn to equate a lab coat with medical authority. So ditch the ambivalence and take control.

4. Playing Karate instead of Judo

As a business owner, clients will inevitably throw stuff at you. In Karate, the defensive tactic is to block the incoming hits and try not to get hurt. Instead, you want to use the Judo philosophy by taking the attacker's energy and putting it where you want it. Use 'Got it, nevertheless' to redirect the conversation. Instead of blocking, set up your processes so you don't have to overcome objections repeatedly. When a prospect complains about a long treatment plan, say, "Yes, remember we talked about this time-frame on the phone." Play Judo, taking the energy that is thrown at you and putting it where you want it.

5. Blaming or shaming the client

The last thing you want to do in the sales environment is blame or shame the client in any way. Their problem may have been of their own creating through neglect or stupidity, but you don't need to point it out. Remove any language such as, "If you had only followed the instructions in the owner's manual" or "You would feel a lot different if you had stuck to your diet." We sometimes use a form of blame in order to create a bond with people, as in "I know, I totally did that stupid thing, too," but we should cut out this language as well. Imagine that you are an airline pilot on a plane that is crashing. You would not get on the loudspeaker with a crazed voice and freak out. Don't break your professional rapport. Instead, calmly instruct your clients to put their heads down and brace for impact. Blaming behavior is not endearing to you. When you use it, your clients will become motivated by fear of loss and disconnect with you. Use inspiration. Show them what they can have or become, and they will aspire to that new reality.

6. Expecting to deliver perfection

When the expectation is perfection, there is a problem. Remember, if you are a self-proclaimed perfectionist, you are really an imperfectionist. You are constantly looking for what is wrong. Stop it! Develop the expectation that you will deliver the best possible outcome. When you expect perfection and then tell people that you might not be able to deliver flawlessness, you put the burden on them. Instead of striving for the best possibility, you are projecting on them that if they don't do their part right, they are wrong. I love the mantra of excellence. We deliver excellence. It will always be a journey, and there will always be room for improvements, so shoot for excellence and allow for the continued learning that will come.

RAPID Selling Framework

My goal throughout this book has been to share with you as many ways you can improve your sales process and increase the amount of people who say 'Yes' to you. For the last section of this book I want to share with you my favorite sales system of all time.

Kevin Nations is one of the highest-level sales experts and coaches in the world. I had the privilege of being coached by him for a year back in 2014. The following is an overview of his selling framework that is literally responsible for hundreds of millions of dollars in sales. What I love about the systems is it's not only applicable for sales, but for all areas of your life. Instead of a "tactic" or a "sales strategy," the system is different because it allows you to have straightforward and open interactions with your clients.

The RAPID system offers so much transparency that closing conversations become incredibly smooth. I personally have used it to close millions of dollars in sales inside my business as well as commitments from others that have nothing to do with a financial exchange, but a relationship exchange instead. It has created dramatic results for my clients and within my own business as well.

RAPID will help you: Recognize why you are really here, Ask questions that move you forward, Probe for the real problem, Investigate a solution, make a Decision with a deadline.

R - Recognize
A - Ask
P - Probe for Problems
I - Investigate
D - Decision with a Deadline

Let's start with the most important and usually the most avoided conversation in the process, recognizing why you are both in the room.

Recognize

From the very outset of the RAPID system, you connect with the client by Recognizing. You verbally recognize why you as a businessperson and the client as a consumer are meeting here together. I know it may sound like a no-brainer, but articulating the intentions of each party and what the appointment is about clarifies and opens up the conversation. You are not initially there for the same reason.

For most of your prospective clients, they will be meeting with you to gather information. They will be curious about what you do, they might want to participate, or they are there to get the details in order to make a decision. However, as a salesperson, your intent is to figure out if what you do is a fit for this person so you can take the next step with your service, i.e. Close the Deal. The Recognize step allows you to clear the playing field and let your prospects know where you stand. You will find that your clients appreciate this recognition. Instead of having to tiptoe around the sales aspect of the conversation, you can both understand that you are meeting for a decision to be made.

"Hey Lisa, I want to thank you so much for being here with me today. I just want to recognize right off the top why we're both here. I totally understand that you're here to gather some information to see if working with Dr. Roman would be the best benefit for you. I'm here to help us so at the end of this process we can both have a decision made so we can move on with our lives. Does that sound okay to you?"

Ask

In this step, you outline for the prospect what the sales presentation is going to look like. It's almost like a trial close to help them understand that you are looking for a decision at the end. You inform them that you are going to **ask** some questions to see if you are a good fit, they can **ask** any questions they want during the presentation, and then at the end you will **ask** them to decide one way or another. You ask them, they ask you, and then you ask during the close. The Ask step allows you to stay in control of the conversation and guide the client toward a decision at the end.

"I just want to ask you some questions to see if or how we can help you. I'll tell you about our services, and you can ask any questions you like, then just tell me if this makes sense or not. Is that fair?"

Probing for Pain

Probing for pain means finding out what people want. You want to find the thing that was so painful that they would take time out of their lives to come to you. Though you don't want to become their shrink and have people crying through the screen at you, you do want to probe deep enough to uncover the root of the pain that you can fix.

Remember that people buy emotionally and justify with logic, so the closer you can get to their emotional rationale the better. People buy things they want. Other than the basics, people often don't even buy what they need. When you can connect with a client and uncover their emotional pain, you're on the right track.

I've watched about five minutes of the show Nip/Tuck, which documents patients during their plastic surgery experience. I wasn't interested in the rest of the show, but they ask prospective clients a question every time that is so brilliant. The doctors always ask, "What do you hate about the way you look?" It works well in that plastic surgery space to help their clientele pinpoint their pain. I'm not advocating that you ask people what they hate. We want to help people open up about their pain without the self-loathing. A simple "What's your biggest challenge?" works much better.

Probing for pain can be tricky because many of us will answer a negative question with a justified, positive answer. When someone asks us, "What's your biggest challenge?" (negative), we answer with, "Well, things really aren't that bad" (positive). People often justify their pain. For example, someone whose pain is that they really want to lose weight will also say they are super busy and don't want to go to the gym and really like peanut M&Ms. When you are probing for someone's pain, they return to their comfort zone where things aren't that bad. This is often referred to as RTF, Return to Fine. Sometimes a client will talk for quite a while and talk themselves out of their pain. Be careful of RTF because your clients won't want to spend money if they are fine. When one of my clients does this, I thank them for telling me it's okay, but then I redirect them back to the reason they scheduled with me, and that's their pain. I let them know that I help people get out of pain. As you zoom in on the deeper reasons behind why they want what they want, take note of as many pain points as you can so you can help them move past their pain.

"So tell me Lisa, what is the biggest challenge you are facing right now when it comes to your smile?"

Investigate

In this RAPID system step, you are going to allow the client to investigate what the outcome will look like if they choose to work with you. You want to encourage them to open up to the possibility of a future free from their pain through your expertise. We are living in a world full of a lot of choices, and in this step you want them to start investigating how their life would change if they chose you. You want them to figure it out on their own because it will be much more powerful if they are envisioning it for themselves.

Leading up to this step, you'll include plenty of evidence that your services provide the answer to the client's pain. Modify your presentation to address their specific needs and showcase your expertise. Using visuals helps to jump-start the client's positive expectations of the future, so use customized case studies and visual evidence before you ask the client to investigate the outcome.

"So Lisa, what have you done up to this point to manage your teeth? With all of the options that you have out there, why would you choose us to help give you the smile you've been dreaming of? Once you get to a point where you know your smile is being transformed by our team, how will you feel? What will that help open up for you in your life? Paint the picture for me of what that end result looks like for you."

Decision with a Deadline

If you have not yet incorporated a deadline into your sales close, today is the day to make that change. When you give people a deadline, they will act. You can package a deadline into a limited-time pricing promotion or a down-payment matching program. Offer to knock a certain percentage off the price or to match the client's down-payment if they close by the end of the day and see your same-day closes skyrocket. A deadline defends the investment they are making, and matching gives them an immediate benefit from their investment.

"Lisa, here's what we've got going on here. We can help you with that smile treatment, and we can do it for a price of $6,000. As I mentioned in the beginning I'm looking for a 'yes' or 'no' decision today. Both 'yes' and 'no' are perfectly good answers, I'm not going to make you feel bad or chase you down or anything like that. However, if you decide to move forward today I will scholarship you and bring that price down to $5,500. What do you think?"

The RAPID selling framework (Recognize, Ask, Probe for Pain, Investigate, and Decision with a Deadline) is a powerful way to close. You can use the steps to craft a quick and easy sales presentation, or you can weave each step into your existing process. Decide how you are going to incorporate this framework and then roleplay the heck out of it so it flows from you naturally. The entire RAPID framework can fit into a quick 5-minute conversation. Here's an example:

"I'm Dr. Hardy and I'm here to make sure we have the right treatment for you. I know you're probably here to gather some information. We're here to help you make a better decision. I'm going to ask you a few questions, and then you can ask me any questions you like during our time, but in the end I know that Christine is going to ask you for a decision one way or another. Is that okay? Great. What is the biggest challenge you have when it comes to your teeth? What bothers you most about your smile? Thank you for sharing that. What would it be like if that challenge were no longer a problem? When we are able to fix it, what will that change for you? How will you feel in 18 months when you have this new smile? Great. We have some time to get you into the chair today to get your first scan completed and get your treatment going. I'll let Christine take over so she can work with you on making that decision."

Afterword

There was a time when your days, weeks and months were highly scheduled and regulated. You had gotten comfortable with the busy-ness of business, the routine and the predictability. Perhaps you had arrived at a place in your life where you went along with the day before you unintentionally.

Could you have ever imagined what might happen if the world stopped? What if schools and businesses everywhere simply stopped, and the planet was able to take a breath? What if you were able to start anew and reconsider the flow of your life? What if you could turn away from what you never missed and embrace something even better? This season is a tremendous opportunity.

Before this year shook your foundations, you may have been in a state of **Unconscious Incompetence** when it comes to virtual exams. You likely were unaware or only vaguely familiar with the virtual business world and your lack of proficiency. Once Covid knocked the unconsciousness out of us, suddenly we knew about virtual and its value. You likely progressed to **Conscious Incompetence**, where you are aware of the skill but not yet proficient. You may have experienced this when you first went live on social media with your story. As you read this book and completed the challenges, you are experiencing **Conscious Competence**, where you are able to use the skill but only with effort. My hope for you is that you continue to progress and become fluent in virtual sales and exams, achieving **Unconscious Competence**. Performing the skill will become automatic and be so ingrained in your business that it no longer presents problems for you. Each stage in the Competence cycle is okay to be in, as long as you are willing to take the next step.

My son-in-law, Sam, has been colorblind all of this life. He never complained about the lack of color in a sunset or his inability to match his pairs of socks because his visual perspective was all he ever knew. My daughter decided to surprise him with a pair of glasses that would allow him to see more of the colors that she could see, allowing him to enter her world of vivid color. If you've seen the YouTube videos of babies being able to hear for the first time or grown men being able to see the world in full color, you can imagine Sam's reaction when my daughter placed the glasses over his eyes. He could finally see what shades of green really looked like and how different pink is from gray.

Though Sam doesn't wear the glasses all of the time, they do allow him to see things he wasn't able to see before. He finally understood what everyone else was perceiving, and it turned him on to opportunities to experience this planet in new ways. Before, he simply had no idea what he was missing.

In my mind, I see many parallels between Sam's experience of being able to see with new eyes and the call for you to embrace virtual sales. I know that many of you are doing just fine with your present sales practices and in-person services. However, once you experience the color of virtual and see how many opportunities it provides, you'll never see things the same again. Virtual can open up your time and expand your connections with team members and clients in a way that no other tactic can match. It will give you a whole new business world to see.

Digital is not going away. The question is, ten years from now, are you going to look back and wish that you had put on the virtual glasses sooner? As you implement these virtual ideas in your office, you will shift your culture and the way people show up for you. I've watched businesses become transformed through a few small adjustments, and it means the world to me to be a part of it. I hope this book has inspired you to get creative and embrace a different way of serving your clients. If my work helps you get one new client, or helps you build a stronger connection with your team members, or creates more value in your business, or strengthens your ties to your spouse or kids, then I call that a win. Thank you for allowing me to be a part of your journey!

My Virtual Start

I love sales. I geek out about it on so many levels. I'm always on the lookout for new ways to present a product or new language to help people move past their hang ups. Sales is the drive that wakes me up in the middle of the night with a new idea and then gets me out of bed in the morning.

But I know everyone is not built this way.

As I was writing this book, this thought kept running through my mind. I wanted to create something that could help you transition into the virtual exam space and stay relevant without heaping one more job on you. I don't want practices watching the virtual transition go by and having to play catchup later.

My Virtual Start is an orthodontic sales service specializing in Virtual Patient Acquisitions. With the help of a team of Invisible Treatment Coordinators, we contract with practices to generate local leads, perform a virtual screening process for prospective patients, and ultimately deliver down payments and contracts.

At My Virtual Start we work hand-in-hand with each doctor, matching every practice with a Dino Watt sales-certified Invisible TC who uses *your* branding and culture to guide the virtual sales process. Doctors are involved in every step of the process, including providing a one minute diagnosis for each case which you can complete from your smart device. You can offload your start acquisitions process and let My Virtual Start do some of the heavy lifting for you.

Every industry has a graveyard of businesses that were built up, flourished, and then lost their relevance. In 1997 (clear) aligners were introduced, and the critics said they would never be effective. In 2010 same-day starts came up on the dental radar, and they said good doctors needed more time than that to plan. Well, it's 2021, and the virtual exam is here to stay. If you want to stay relevant without upending your current processes, ask for a demo at www.MyVirtualStart.com.

Dino's Best Reads

Ask by Ryan Levesque

Change Your Brain, Change Your Life: the breakthrough program for conquering anxiety, depression, obsessiveness, anger and impulsiveness by Daniel G. Amen

Closer's Survival Guide by Grant Cardone

Communicate Excellence: A Guide to Authentic, Positive, Consistent Front Desk Communication by Amy Demas

The Go-Giver: A Little Story About a Powerful Business Idea by Bob Burg and John David Mann

How to Win Friends and Influence People by Dale Carnegie

Influence: The Psychology of Persuasion by Robert Cialdini

Limitless: upgrade your brain, learn anything faster, and unlock your exceptional life by Jim Qwik

Never Split the Difference: negotiating as if your life depended on it by Chris Voss

No: The Only Negotiating System You Need for Work or Home by Jim Camp

The Only Negotiating Guide You'll Ever Need: 101 Ways to Win Every Time in Any Situation by Peter B. Stark and Jane Flaherty

Personality Isn't Permanent by Benjamin Hardy

Pre-Suasion: A Revolutionary Way to Influence and Persuade by Robert Cialdini

The Power of Habit by Charles Duhigg

The Road Less Stupid: Advice from the Chairman of the Board by Keith J. Cunningham

The 7 Habits of Highly Effective People by Steven R. Covey

The 7 Principles for Making Marriage Work by John Gottman

The Science of Selling: Proven Strategies to Make Your Pitch, Influence Decisions, and Close the Deal by David Hoffeld

www.ingramcontent.com/pod-product-compliance
Lightning Source LLC
Chambersburg PA
CBHW070350200326
41518CB00012B/2199